300

Waltrip

RACKET SQUAD

BOOKS BY JOHN CHRISTOPHER FINE

Sunken Ships and Treasure
Oceans in Peril
The Hunger Road
Creatures of the Sea
Racket Squad

RACKET SQUAD

John Christopher Fine

Atheneum · 1993 · New York

Maxwell Macmillan Canada
Toronto
Maxwell Macmillan International
New York   Oxford   Singapore   Sydney

Atheneum
Macmillan Publishing Company
866 Third Avenue
New York, NY 10022

Maxwell Macmillan Canada, Inc.
1200 Eglinton Avenue East
Suite 200
Don Mills, Ontario M3C 3N1

Macmillan Publishing Company is part of the Maxwell Communication Group of Companies.

First edition

Printed in the United States of America

10 9 8 7 6 5 4 3 2 1

The text of this book is set in 12/15 Times Roman.

Book design by Sarah Gonzalez Lauck

Fine, John Christopher.
Racket squad / by John Christopher Fine.—1st ed.
p.   cm.
Includes index.
Summary: The author describes how he investigated the role of organized crime in such areas as Medicaid fraud and toxic waste treatment.
ISBN 0-689-31569-4
1. Organized crime—New York (State)—Juvenile literature.
2. Organized crime—New Jersey—Juvenile literature.
3. Racketeering—New York (State)—Juvenile literature.
4. Racketeering—New Jersey—Juvenile literature. 5. Criminal investigation—New York (State)—Juvenile literature. 6. Criminal investigation—New Jersey—Juvenile literature. [1. Organized crime. 2. Criminal investigation.] I. Title.
HV6452.N7F56   1993
364.1'06'09747—dc20   92-5199

CONTENTS

1

RACKET SQUAD

What are criminal gangs but petty kingdoms?

A gang is a group of men under the command of a leader, bound by compact of association, in which the plunder is divided according to an agreed convention. If this villainy wins so many recruits that it acquires territory, establishes a base, captures cities, and subdues people, it then openly arrogates to itself the title of kingdom, which is conferred on it in the eyes of the world, not by the renouncement of aggression but by the attainment of impunity.

Saint Augustine, *The City of God*, circa A.D. 412

Gangsters, racketeers, mobsters, organized crime figures, made men, wise guys. The Mafia, la Cosa Nostra, the Syndicate, the Black Hand Society, the Crime Cartel. All of these terms present mental images. Sometimes these images are exaggerated by film producers to take advantage of people's attraction to violence. Some of these images are sensationalized by newspaper headlines. All of these images have one thing in common: power. Organized crime, at its very root, is power—power to accumulate wealth and, with that wealth, to buy protection. Wealth protects outlaws from rivals and from the law.

There is hardly a better definition of organized crime than Saint Augustine's description, yet the search for a definition has been a major undertaking of United States lawmakers and law enforcers for decades. Even an attorney general of the United States, called to testify before Congress, was unable to define organized crime when asked the following questions during a 1978 hearing on fraud and racketeering in Medicare and Medicaid:

> ATTORNEY GENERAL GRIFFIN B. BELL: I don't know myself. I would like to say that I don't know for sure what organized crime is.
> CONGRESSMAN MARKS: Excuse me a minute. You are telling us you don't know what organized crime is?
> ATTORNEY GENERAL BELL: I don't know what the definition is. I suppose if you were to see the facts, you would know it as you might know whether something was obscene or not. You would have a feeling about it.

While there may have been some logic in the attorney general's comments at the time of his testimony, there certainly were laws on the books that defined many of the racketeering and organized criminal activities. What was apparent from the testimony of the chief law enforcement officer of the United States was the overall need for professional law enforcement to come to grips with a problem that has plagued America since the days of the first colonization.

There have been criminal gangs throughout the history

of America. They robbed stagecoaches and trains, held up banks, organized badlands, owned towns in the gold boom eras, offered services in everything from baths to brothels, trafficked in all manner of contraband, and offered protection for a price in places where no civilized law controlled human conduct. As new immigrants flocked to America's shores, ethnic gangs preyed upon newcomers, who were ignorant of the laws, customs, and language. The new immigrants were weak and afraid. Yielding to their fears, they were forced to pay extortion money to the gangs for protection.

Throughout the history of organized crime in America, there has been a parallel in law enforcement. The United States marshal, Texas ranger, treasury agent, and special district attorney—all have played roles in combating organized crime, responding to specific crises in lawlessness.

Today in the United States, racketeering is largely prosecuted at the federal level under laws originally passed in 1968 as the Federal Safe Streets Act, which was expanded by the 1970 law called the Federal Organized Crime Control Act. Chapter 96 of this law is called Racketeer Influenced and Corrupt Organizations, known as the RICO statute. Many other federal statutes make specific conduct engaged in by organized criminals unlawful, and a number of states have their own version of RICO statutes. Under RICO, racketeering activity is defined as "any act or threat involving murder, kidnapping, gambling, arson, robbery, bribery, extortion, dealing in obscene matter, or dealing in narcotic or other dangerous drugs, which is chargeable under state law and punishable by imprisonment for more than one year." RICO goes on to list a whole series of federal crimes including murder-for-hire, sexual exploitation of children, embezzlement of union funds, and violations of the Currency and Foreign Transactions Reporting Act (where ill-gotten gains are laundered, their sources and origins are disguised, and the money or other forms of currency are taken out of the country or not reported on federal forms).

In defining the characteristics of organized crime, the United States Law Enforcement Assistance Administration's Task Force on Organized Crime reported: "Organized crime is a type of conspiratorial crime, sometimes involving the hierarchical coordination of a number of persons in the planning and execution of illegal acts, or in the pursuit of a legitimate objective by unlawful means. Organized crime involves continuous commitment by key members. . . ."

The task force recognized that organized crime's "conspiratorial groups are usually very quick and effective in controlling and disciplining their members, associates, and victims. Therefore, organized crime participants are unlikely to disassociate themselves from the conspiracies and are in the main incorrigible." The task force stated that "organized crime is not synonymous with the Mafia or la Cosa Nostra, the most experienced, diversified, and possibly best disciplined of the conspiratorial groups. The Mafia image is a common stereotype of organized crime members. Although a number of families of la Cosa Nostra are an important component of organized crime operations, they do not enjoy a monopoly on underworld activities."

In all of the definitions, federal and state, there is a common thread that seems to return to the basic description by Saint Augustine, written more than fifteen hundred years ago. That common thread will be found throughout *Racket Squad*. It is a book of cases and examples of organized criminal activity chosen not so much from

District Attorney Frank S. Hogan being sworn in by Supreme Court Justice Mollen. In the background is a photograph of Thomas Dewey.

within a framework of strict definitions of what is and what may not be organized crime, but from some of the cases that were the author's day-to-day work as prosecutor and investigator in federal, state, and local systems of government. This book describes the work of the Racket Squad, District Attorney Frank S. Hogan's legendary office in the county of New York, and the author's hands-on accounts of cases he handled.

The present ideas of rackets prosecution began in 1935, when New York's governor, Herbert H. Lehman, appointed an assistant prosecutor from the United States District Attorney's office to head a special investigation. Organized crime was active, and corruption was widespread in public office. Criminals controlled political figures. A grand jury was called to investigate the activities of Charles "Lucky" Luciano and Dutch Schultz and their connection to the numbers gambling racket and the corrupt Democratic politicians in control. The jury became angered by the failure of the district attorney (DA) to provide them with proof of wrongdoing and demanded they be given the evidence. County district attorneys in New York, with their assistants, serve as counsel to grand juries. When it became apparent to the grand jury in New York County (the borough of Manhattan) that the district attorney was not acting as they wished, the grand jurors took unprecedented action on their own and forced the governor of New York to name a special prosecutor.

In order to understand the district attorney's function before a grand jury, a short explanation of what a grand jury is and how it functions may be helpful. The grand jury in New York State, composed of twenty-three ordinary citizens, hears evidence presented by the prosecutor and sometimes by a defendant. It has the power to return an indictment, which means it charges the accused with a crime. The accused then must stand trial before a petit jury, which determines innocence or guilt. A grand jury can also dismiss charges against a person arrested by the police. In many jurisdictions, a grand jury has the authority to report to a court about matters of concern, such as incompetence or corruption in public office. In some states, grand juries have jurisdiction to inspect public institutions such as prisons and mental hospitals.

The wide-ranging jurisdiction of a grand jury, coupled with its subpoena power—which requires witnesses to come before it and compels their truthful testimony—makes it one of the most important weapons in the war against organized crime. Failure to attend and honor a grand jury subpoena is a serious matter and may result in indictment for contempt. Failure to answer questions before a grand jury may also subject the witness to contempt charges. In New York, for example, a conviction for contempt may bring a four-year prison term. Not telling the truth before a grand jury is a serious offense, subjecting the witness in New York to penalties of up to seven years in prison.

There are various forms of immunity from prosecution that are available to witnesses who are compelled to answer questions before grand juries. Under the federal and most state constitutions, people cannot be made to testify or provide evidence that would tend to incriminate themselves. To encourage their testimony, witnesses are granted immunity, so that their own testimony cannot be used against them.

Immunity can take many forms. "Blanket immunity" gives the person testifying permanent immunity from prosecution; "transactional immunity" covers only the transaction discussed in testimony; and "use immunity" means the evidence obtained from the compelled testimony cannot be used against the person, but a person can still be prosecuted if there is other evidence of criminal activity. The law of immunity is complex, and it varies widely from state to state and within the federal system.

This background information should provide a clearer understanding of how a rackets investigation functions before a grand jury. The Racket Squad and district attorney obtain evidence through informants, surveillance, electronic eavesdropping, search warrants, and police work, and present it to a grand jury. Witnesses are compelled to attend the grand jury and testify under subpoena. The grand jury then is used as an "investigative tool," developing the evidence.

Responding to the furor raised by the New York County Grand Jury and a mounting scandal of corruption, Governor Lehman appointed Thomas E. Dewey as special prosecutor. Dewey rose to fame during the course of his rackets-busting investigations and was later to become governor of New York and then presidential candidate running against Harry S Truman. Dewey was sworn in as special prosecutor on July 29, 1935, with seven other men, including Frank S. Hogan and Alfred J. Scotti.

Dewey later won election to the office of district attorney of New York County in 1937 and continued his rackets busting, putting an end to corrupt clubhouse politics and political appointments in the district attorney's office. One bureau created in the district attorney's office was the Rackets Bureau, which dealt with organized crime and political corruption. It was staffed with top prosecutors. New York City detectives were handpicked for the DA's Racket Squad. They were men who could be counted on for specialized skills, integrity, intelligence, and dedication. The office added certified public accounts who, as investigative accountants, would go with squad detectives on raids to seize account books and records of bookmakers, loan sharks, and union bosses, analyzing them to prove illegalities. In the early rackets-busting days, corruption was so widespread and flagrant that investigators often found notations right on the books for payoffs to police and public figures.

The DA's office also hired its own staff of rackets investigators. These men defied even the most careful police spotter by their appearance and manner. They worked under cover, infiltrating the mob, and on police corruption cases when it was not wise to test the loyalty of other New York City policemen by asking them to gather evidence against other cops.

Special Prosecutor Dewey, then District Attorney Dewey, began a new concept in law enforcement. In 1941, when he was succeeded by Hogan, one of the men on his staff, the Dewey concept and the integrity of the DA's office were assured. Like Dewey before him, Hogan became a legend, elected to eight successive four-year terms. Hogan remained in office until 1973, when a stroke forced him to resign. Hogan then appointed Scotti as head of the Rackets Bureau. Scotti was later named chief assistant district attorney, while continuing to serve as Rackets Bureau head. Promotion within Hogan's office was by seniority, a system to insure that assistant district attorneys rose through the office ranks on the basis of merit and not politics.

Hogan had several ironclad rules for his assistant DAs and other employees. These rules were based not only on experience during the Dewey investigations into corruption in the prosecutor's office, but on the demand for integrity in the DA's office as well. Assistants were not permitted to go to racetracks or nightclubs, normal hangouts of organized crime gamblers and underworld figures. Political activity of any kind was prohibited. Assistant DAs were recruited from the nation's top law schools. Only rarely did Hogan hire lawyers who had already been working in other jobs. Then, regardless of their experience, they always started with the entering class of law graduates, without any special advantage. Hogan preferred to hire assistants who had attained top law school honors and also had worked their way through school, people with varied backgrounds but usually those who were born and brought up in New York City.

Ingrained into the new assistants were certain important rules, which were established to maintain the integrity of the office. The rules included these points:

1. Assistants were not to shake hands in court with defense lawyers. Experience showed that some defense lawyers in criminal courts were corrupt and often returned to their clients, after shaking hands with prosecutors, to tell the defendants that the assistant DAs had been bribed and it would cost the clients additional fees.

2. Assistants were never to enter the jail area behind the courtrooms, where inmates were kept before they were brought before the court for action on their cases. Inmates later might claim they had bribed the assistant DA or that the assistant DA had told them they would receive a lesser sentence during the conversation held in the secrecy of the court pen. DAs who could swear that they never entered the pens had far better credentials than those who might try to explain that a conversation had been misunderstood by a defendant.

3. Courtesy was stressed. Telephone calls were re-

turned promptly and mail was answered; assistants behaved politely in and out of court.

4. Frank Hogan read all of the mail that came into the DA's office—he read everything, no matter to whom it was addressed. He did this every day to keep track of court motions and any problems, and so that he could query individual assistants or their bureau chiefs about matters that concerned him. No letter or legal paper left the DA's office unless it was approved by the bureau chief and a copy initialed by the supervisor. A skilled staff of clerks kept cards on every piece of correspondence that ever came in or went out of the office, providing a permanent record of complaints and correspondents.

5. Assistants were required to make a four-year commitment, and any who left before their four-year term was up incurred the displeasure of Frank Hogan, which often meant he would not write letters of recommendation for them.

Hogan's office was a ministry of justice. Absolute integrity, idealistic assistants dedicated to public service, and capable staff members meant that an equal degree of pride was taken in clearing an innocent person as in convicting the guilty. A defense lawyer never hesitated to inform the DA when he thought his client was being framed or unjustly accused.

The first words this author heard, stepping through the doorway of Hogan's detective unit after joining the office, were those of large, burly Detective First Grade Nick Barrett, answering a telephone. Detective Barrett's deep baritone voice echoed across the room as he spoke into the receiver. "Racket Squad," he said, a memorable name for a legend that symbolized the fight for justice against corruption and organized crime.

Racket Squad traces many famous cases and investigations of organized crime, racketeering, and gang activities—cases that, in their truth, are more dramatic than any fiction.

2
RACKETEERS

They are professional criminals. They live by their own code and behave according to their own rules. Romanticized by grotesque Hollywood versions of godfathers and described by Italian words taken from congressional hearings, the modern organized crime figure is actually more a business-man than the thug who prowls the piers with a lead pipe, such as the gangster in the film version of *On the Waterfront*. Today's mobsters have adapted themselves to sophisticated business techniques, which, for all intents and purposes, give them an aura of respectability. But beyond that, nothing has changed. The use of brutality and murder by the mob to enforce its will and code of conduct continues.

By its very nature, the political system lends itself to corruption. Politicians must start at local political clubs doing menial tasks such as licking envelopes and running errands before they are given money-earning appointments as guard-ians or custodians—in the case of lawyers—or receive any of the paid appointments in government. The "big time" comes much later in political careers. The political clubhouse tests a newcomer; few American politicians come away clean. There are always favors, payoffs, contributions, and temptations, and always the possibility of scoring big someday.

In the wake of a massive police corruption scandal in New York City, which revealed organized criminal payoffs to the police, the city appointed a special anticorruption prosecutor. This prosecutor stated publicly that judges in New York buy their jobs. This statement was probably more true than false, given New York City's history of back-room political deals.

What Special Prosecutor Maurice Nadjari said about the courts applies to the entire political system. Political power often is traded as a commodity. Influence pedaling, or the ability to get a politician to pull strings to accomplish something for a secret payoff, has always been part of the underworld's system of organized corruption. Since these conspiracies are secret, often accomplished with only a word in the right person's ear, detection is difficult or impossible.

The racketeers' code of silence, called *omerta,* a word of Italian origin made famous during early United States Senate hearings on organized crime, is absolute. Corrupt police will not ordinarily conspire with street punks. The police know that if the criminals are arrested, they will trade any information they have for lighter sentences, including the fact that they paid off the police. Historically, though, the racketeer never talks, a guarantee enforced by blood. The ironclad guarantee is the reason organized crime figures can be relied upon to keep silent about dealings with police and public figures. In the corrupt system dominated by organized crime, the penalty for disloyalty is death. That is how organized crime took hold in the United States and why it flourishes. Racketeers also have the money needed to finance political campaigns and to funnel cash into the pockets of district leaders.

In the annals of organized crime, a few gangsters stand out: Charles "Lucky" Luciano, Al Capone, Frank Costello, Albert Anastasia, Joe Colombo, and Anthony "Fat Tony" Salerno. In their own ways, they have left marks on American history. Indeed, investigations of two of the organized crime bosses and their associates during my tenure in District Attorney Frank Hogan's Rackets Bureau demonstrated the mob's power and influence, the secret lives of its members, as well as their public images. For all of their sophistication, one thing was always eminently clear: They were ruthless criminals, who were uncommonly good at their trade, and whose crimes affected everyone.

JOE COLOMBO

"The face is very blue, the eyes are bulging, and the tongue protrudes between the teeth. . . . Marks of decomposition are already noted on the anterior chest wall. . . . There is evidence of bleeding from the nares on his body. Eyes show presence of a definite subconjunctival hemorrhage. There is a cord around this body's neck knotted in the front twice around the neck and two strands on the right side. There is a loop formed by knotting the cord and it is tightly drawn around the neck."

The police report and autopsy by the city medical examiner detailed the double homicide of Anthony "Nino" Colombo and his apparent mistress, Christina Oliveri. Their bodies were found together on February 6, 1938.

Murdered bodies of Joe Colombo's father, Anthony, and a female companion

Anthony "Nino" Colombo, alias Toney Durante, alias Toney Colombo, was a petty thug. At forty-two, he had a police record that included arrests for robbery, extortion, and assault, possession of a pistol, burglary, disorderly conduct, and vagrancy. When the police interrogated Colombo's wife, Catherine, she told them, "I always had trouble with my husband about women. He went out and I went to the movies. That's the last I saw of him. I figured he was brought in in the roundup and I thought nothing of it."

The two bodies, found covered with oilcloth in the rear of Colombo's Pontiac, had been dead three days. Both had been beaten on the head and murdered by strangulation, the sash cords drawn tightly around their necks. The hom-

16

icides of Anthony "Nino" Colombo and Christina Oliveri went unsolved, eventually fading into the dust of police record rooms, updated only routinely after the usual mob suspects were questioned. Thirty-three years later, Anthony Colombo's son, mob boss Joseph Colombo, met a similar fate, gunned down in New York as he was leading an Italian Anti-Defamation League rally. Shot in the head, Joe Colombo never regained consciousness, lingering in a vegetative state until his death seven years later. Joe Colombo's assailant was killed at the scene by Colombo supporters, but who ordered these hits, and why, are still mysteries.

Joe Colombo, head of one of the world's most powerful organized crime gangs, was a modern mob boss: dapper, suave, well mannered, and well dressed. He had a flair and a charisma that many who rose in the ranks of organized crime lacked. The Colombo Family, as federal law enforcement organized crime experts termed his mob, was one of five "families," or organized crime gangs, that controlled New York and New Jersey rackets. However, Colombo's influence and power extended well beyond the boundaries of Brooklyn, New York, where he was based, for Joe Colombo was on the council of an international syndicate of organized crime, which controlled mob activities worldwide.

Colombo was a real estate salesman, having obtained a license from the New York State Department of State. The State Department had held a hearing to determine Colombo's suitability in character and fitness for this license. Colombo was put under oath and made to testify about his activities and criminal record. (Racketeers have to show legitimate sources of income, because federal tax investigators carefully check those who spend money but who either do not file tax returns or falsify sources of income.)

It was Peter Andreoli, the senior district attorney in the Rackets Bureau, who gave me Colombo's testimony. Andreoli said, "Try this. Read it. If you can make a case [against Colombo], tell Al Scotti, and it's yours."

The first step was to speak with Inspector Paul Vitrano, boss of the Racket Squad. He came down with Detective Joseph San Pietro, and we outlined how best to build a case against Colombo for having lied under oath during the State Department hearing. Detective San Pietro was a perfect match for the case, but then, Inspector Vitrano had a special talent for matching up cases with detectives and assistant DAs. San Pietro had fine, old-world manners and was calm and methodical. Whether he was talking to a mobster or a judge, his manner didn't change. He was an experienced police detective and knew the area of Brooklyn where the Colombo mob hung out. He also knew many of the mobsters by sight.

Once the case was assigned, the inspector left us to it, receiving reports from San Pietro as we progressed. Little by little, we assembled evidence showing how Colombo had used his real estate license as a front for his underworld activities. He had lied about important matters both on the written application and at the State Department hearing. We probed the activities of the Colombo mob, hauling many of the gang members before a grand jury, including customers that had dealt with Colombo both as a real estate salesman and as a car salesman for a Brooklyn Buick dealership. The investigation provided valuable knowledge of the gang members and their criminal activities, as well as of the fronts they were using to conceal their activities and account for their cash.

The police action put pressure on the gang by interrupting the ventures that masked their illegal activities. People were afraid of being indicted and so went to Colombo to complain. Colombo's lawyers then called the police and announced that their client wanted to provide information. It was decided to invite them to discuss the matter.

In all of his dealings, Colombo was well-spoken, articulate, and, like Detective San Pietro, gentlemanly. We were given further access to records and information by Colombo's real estate associates and were asked to please stop subpoenaing their customers since it was injuring the business.

Joe Colombo was indicted for perjury. Detective San Pietro and members of the Racket Squad arrested him at the site of his Brooklyn real estate company. He was brought in and asked whether he had anything to say. With his usual good manners, the impeccably dressed Colombo declined

Police mug shot of crime boss Joseph Colombo

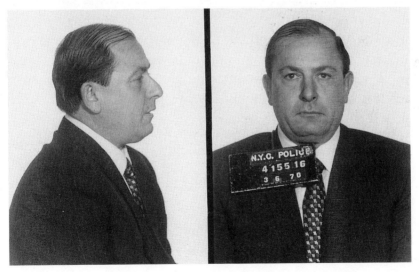

19

to cooperate. Detective San Pietro took Colombo upstairs to the squad room, where he was fingerprinted. Then he was taken around to the Fifth Precinct, booked, and brought to court for arraignment.

The Colombo case came at a time when the Black Panthers, a militant African-American organization that advocated violence along with increased political power, were protesting arrests and police investigations into their activities.

The courtroom hallways in the criminal courts building were packed with Black Panthers and their supporters. They were posting signs on the walls, passing out handbills that read KILL THE PIGS, and disrupting the functions of the court. As Detective San Pietro escorted Joe Colombo from a courthouse elevator, Colombo then and there hatched a plan that would not only bring him international attention and publicity but fifteen months later would see him shot down in New York, at Columbus Circle.

"Look at them," Colombo said to Detective San Pietro as the two left the elevator and were confronted by hallways filled with Black Panthers. "Me and my lawyers have to behave like gentlemen in court. If we didn't, they'd throw us in jail. But these [expletive deleted] can get away with anything. That's gonna change. Watch and see what we're gonna do," Colombo said.

Colombo was arraigned on the charges, and after posting bail, he was released from jail. When he left the criminal courts building that day, he had worked out his plan for the Italian Anti-Defamation League, a program embracing civil rights, which would become Joe Colombo's sophisticated mob shakedown racket.

Colombo's trial was held in the old supreme court building. The grand marble columns, ornate facade, and wide steps made the building a favorite Hollywood backdrop for courtroom scenes. On trial day, Colombo had sound trucks outside and posters put up. Hundreds of demonstrators picketed outside and then filled the courthouse. Racket Squad detectives had an easy time picking out organized crime figures and their wives and families in the assembled crowds. The courtroom was packed. Uniformed court officers enforced security, searching all persons for weapons before they were allowed to enter.

Seats were assigned, but not by any official declaration or judicial mandate: The Colombo forces had allocated seating to their gang members. It was the first time organized crime figures had come to court so openly, and so the news media had a field day—that is, those reporters who could get seats. One of the squad detectives, who was unknown to the Colombo mob, entered the courtroom and prepared to sit down on an empty bench. A gang member moved in on him and told the detective that the bench was reserved and he would have to leave. Recognizing the thug, the detective identified himself and exchanged words with the man. Nothing more was said, but it was clear that Colombo had orchestrated the events.

Previously, the Federal Organized Crime Strike Force in Brooklyn had attempted to bring Colombo to trial on a federal case, but the trial had been cut short, due in great measure to the new pressures Colombo and his organization had been able to exert. What Joe Colombo had observed the Black Panthers pull off in court—the tactics of intimidation and protest they used so effectively—worked equally well for organized crime. The word *mafia* was dubbed anti-Italian, and many politicians who were in the mob's pocket spoke out about the anti-Italian efforts of law enforcement.

The supreme court judge we drew for our trial usually presided over civil, not criminal, cases. Justice Harold Baer was confident and controlled, learned and flexible. The jury panel was summoned and we began the voir dire, a process whereby the lawyers for both the prosecution and the defense ask potential jurors questions in order to determine whether they can be fair and impartial.

Each day, the jurors had to walk past a gamut of mobsters and their supporters crowding the corridors. One police detective working under cover remarked that he was having an easy time keeping an eye on Colombo gang members because they were in court every day. Things weren't going well for Colombo. The jurors chosen were upstanding members of the community, and mob boss Colombo made it clear he was not satisfied with his attorney. As the jury was impaneled, Colombo switched attorneys, bringing in two others as replacements. This was an obvious stalling tactic, but Judge Baer had no choice but to dismiss the jury panel and summon another one. Finally, when a second twelve-member panel had been chosen, along with alternate jurors, the trial began.

Posters and stickers were being pasted all over the hallways and in court corridors. It was a means of intimidating the jurors, who had to walk past them. A section of the judiciary law makes it a criminal offense to paste up stickers and posters. I requested a conference in chambers with the judge, defense counsel, and Colombo. I quoted the law and told the defense that the district attorney was prepared to enforce the law and institute criminal prosecutions of offenders. Colombo promised that the actions would cease. As I left the courthouse that afternoon I saw Joe Colombo, his keys in hand, scraping off stickers his zealous supporters had pasted on court walls. Colombo had his own code of conduct. While his organized criminal activities were ruthless, there was never a time when he didn't act like a gentleman.

Colombo ran his trial. He knew what he was doing and had his lawyers follow his wishes. Part of my case was based on a meeting Colombo was observed attending with other members of organized crime at the Concord Hotel, in the Catskill Mountains in upstate New York. Colombo had been questioned about this meeting under oath. He had been observed at the Concord by two off-duty New York City detectives. The perjury involved Colombo's falsely answering questions about the meeting in sworn hearing testimony before the New York Department of State. The hearing was to determine Colombo's fitness to be licensed as a real estate broker. It also involved his lying about prior criminal arrests on his application for the real estate broker's license. The evidence about the gangster meeting was critical to those counts in the indictment. Colombo also realized the impact, since his association with high-level gangsters not only tarnished his new image as a civil rights activist and crusader for the rights of Italian Americans, but it chipped away at his facade of respectability.

The first detective testified. He described his observations at the Concord, noting that Colombo had been seated there with John "Sonny" Franzese, Felice "Philly" Vizzari, Charles "Ruby" Stein, Nicholas Maniello, Albert Gallo, Nat Goodman, Lawrence Gallo, and others. When Colombo and the others had recognized the observers as detectives, they had risen from the table and hastily left. On cross-examination by the defense attorneys, the detective was asked about his association with a certain woman. Something was up. The chief investigator for the Brooklyn district attorney's office, it had been reported to our squad, allegedly had an association with Colombo and was going to testify for him. Our chief assistant district attorney, Al Scotti, who suspected corruption in the Brooklyn DA's office, insisted on bringing the investigator in. Al Scotti was in his seventies; he was slender, short, wore a small mustache, and rarely swore, but he breathed fire when he was aroused. He smelled a fix, and when the investigator was brought before him, no dragon ever breathed hotter. The investigator melted; perspiration beaded his forehead; he squirmed under Scotti's interrogation. He had gotten a car from the Buick dealership Colombo was involved with. He now knew what he faced if he betrayed the law he had been sworn to uphold.

The message apparently went back to Colombo, for they never called for the Brooklyn investigator to testify. They did, however, place the detective at the Concord with a girlfriend. That would have been all right except that the detective had omitted it from his report. When the detective finished testifying, it was clear that his former girlfriend would be called by Colombo's lawyers to refute his testimony. Careful documentation showed that Colombo had in fact been convicted of a crime, a matter he had lied about during the State Department hearing, and that he had been arrested not three times, as he had testified, but twelve. He had concealed this evidence of "bad character," which would have disqualified him from becoming a real estate broker in New York.

Then the detective's ex-girlfriend took the stand. Detective San Pietro had done a thorough background check on all aspects of the case, and now his investigations were invaluable. The defense produced photographs of the detective with his girlfriend.

The woman was cross-examined by the prosecution about the upstate meetings. She slipped. Her detective friend had been anxious to get back to New York City and report on the Concord gangland meeting he had observed. In the car, he had spoken enthusiastically with his girlfriend. "He was saying how it was a Little Appalacia meeting," the woman blurted out. The response had its effect. In 1957, police had raided a meeting of underworld hoods in Appalacia, New York, rounding up many of the most notorious gangsters in America. This new upstate meeting with Colombo and the men at the Concord, fewer in number than at the original Appalacia meeting, was indeed a Little Appalacia. In police intelligence terms, it was a significant indication of associations. Colombo's attorneys objected. The court was told that the woman was the defense lawyer's witness and that the prosecution hadn't asked anything about Appalacia. Colombo's lawyers withdrew their objection, probably sorry they had ever called the woman in the first place.

Gangsters never want to take the stand. They never want to testify. Cross-examination permits questioning that can bring out all prior misconduct, including criminal convictions and previous bad conduct in order to discredit a witness's testimony. But Colombo was confident and agreed to testify for himself. He had never been convicted of a serious crime, all of his twelve arrests being for petty offenses. Some had been gangster roundups like those his father, Anthony, had been caught in, where gamblers were charged with disorderly conduct, vagrancy, or the like to scoop them off the street. His early gambling arrests were already the subject of the perjury indictment and had occurred far in the past, where a deliberately faulty memory could prevent effective cross-examination on the subject.

Colombo's file from the State Department included the original signature on the department's written real estate licensing examination. It was clear from examining the signature that it was not Colombo's. A police handwriting expert confirmed this presumption. Colombo had not taken the written examination himself. The forgery was fairly good, but the long investigation and our familiarity with every aspect of Colombo and his gang paid off. "It was like a bombshell," Al Scotti said later. As chief assistant district attorney and an Italian American, he joined the prosecution's table in court, discrediting the claim of Colombo's Italian Anti-Defamation League that he was being persecuted because he was Italian.

Joe Colombo had a memory loss. He was clever and careful. He was caught and he knew it. To answer the questions about not having taken the examination directly would have jeopardized everything, so he simply said he didn't remember. He was lying, and that was made clear by the continued cross-examination. Colombo's lawyers objected over and over again. Colombo waived them off. "Sit down, Jack," or "I want to answer that," he might say, and answer he did, showing the skill and prowess that had propelled him to the most powerful position in organized crime in America.

Forged signature of crime boss Joseph Colombo on top line, with examples of the real signature. The forged signature was on the New York State Department of State real estate license examination, proving that Joseph Colombo never took the examination himself. These exhibits were prepared by police handwriting experts for use at Colombo's trial.

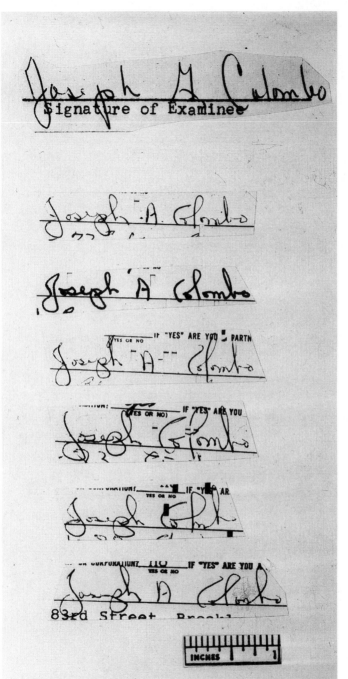

Signature of Examinee

83rd Street Brookl...

INCHES 1

27

Joe Colombo was found guilty of perjury. Finally, one of the world's most notorious racketeers was convicted on felony charges that could put him in prison for up to seven years. He was sentenced to serve from one to two and a half years in prison. But despite my protests, Joe Colombo was released on bail pending his appeal, and he was gunned down in front of thousands of people during his rally at Columbus Circle, New York City.

FAT TONY

Anthony "Fat Tony" Salerno was the king of loan sharks. He controlled New York City's garment district, the hub of fashion for the world market. Nothing moved in the garment district that wasn't controlled by the mob. No trucks, no illegal alien labor, no loans, no gambling, no drugs— nothing. At the center of it all, operating out of the Dunhill Barbershop at 575 Seventh Avenue, was Fat Tony Salerno and his mob. Fat Tony, who lived in a fashionable apartment in Gramercy Park, split his time between New York's garment district, the mob-dominated part of East Harlem, his ranch in the upstate New York community of Rhinebeck, and Florida. While minor racket bosses were princes of the city, Fat Tony was king.

It was a lucky tail. A detective following a petty hoodlum observed a meeting with Fat Tony in an East Harlem section that had remained strictly Italian. Here, blacks from the surrounding poor ghettos were afraid to venture. These were blocks where there was no street crime. To find an area in Harlem where a different kind of fear kept the street safe was only one indication of the mob's power and control. It was thought that Fat Tony had retired from the rackets, yet the squad detective's observations made it clear he was still very much in charge.

Inspector Vitrano mobilized a team of detectives. Surveillance would not be easy, and the only way to break into the mob would be to unravel its pattern of activities through observation. The objective was to gather enough evidence to get a court-authorized warrant for electronic interception. Detectives Dennis Brennan and John O'Rourke were assigned to the case. The investigations would take more than two years and would reveal one of the most widespread criminal financial enterprises operated by organized crime.

Fat Tony was streetwise and clever. He conducted business using a bank of public telephones outside the Dunhill Barbershop, in the garment district. He preferred to talk to his underlings on the street, walking up and down to avoid the possibility of electronic interception. His orders went out through a network of lieutenants, to keep himself isolated from direct contact with those who could incriminate him. Fat Tony smoked big cigars, spoke with the stereotypical mobster's voice, and looked the part of a gangster. He was ruthless, an uncommonly good businessman who made judgments every day in an enterprise that had $80 million outstanding in loan-sharking debts. Our electronic surveillance made this fact a count in Salerno's eventual indictment for criminal usury—providing loans at illegally high interest rates.

Because of the way Salerno and his gang operated, methods had to be devised to enable detectives to overhear their conversations in order to obtain the eavesdropping warrants. Detectives made believe they were using public phones in order to catch segments of Salerno's and his gang members' discussions. Films were made of Salerno's conversations on the street, and expert lip-readers from a school for the deaf were used to interpret them. Salerno's hangouts and apartment premises were kept under surveillance, and his meetings with gang members were monitored.

Although there now was sufficient evidence to warrant a tapping of the public telephones near the Dunhill Barbershop, the task seemed daunting, even for skilled wiremen. It would be impossible to monitor all of the pay phones and impossible to know which ones Fat Tony and his associates would choose for their calls. But since public phones are vandalized routinely in New York City, the wiremen just knocked some of the phones out of commission, limiting the gangsters' selection. Monitoring the phones was one thing; penetrating the gang conspiracies was another. Mobsters are usually circumspect when they speak on any phones, even pay phones. They prefer conversations face-to-face with people they trust.

The investigation revealed that Fat Tony and his associates intended to section off a portion of the Dunhill Barbershop for offices that would serve as their loan headquarters. The new enterprise would be called Merit Commercial and would act as a factoring company, which provides money to and collects the bills for small companies. Charles "Ruby" Stein and Henry Brown would front the operation, and Fat Tony would bankroll it. It was really a loan-sharking operation where borrowers would be charged "vig," or "vigorish," the street slang for interest in excess of 25 percent per year, the legal interest limit in New York. Often the "juice," or interest rates, would go as high as three points (3 percent) or more a week, which would soon add up to more than the original loan. In the garment district, where gambling was rampant and where short-term financing was a way of life, businesses turned to the mob to borrow needed capital.

The evidence began piling up. Court permission was obtained to put a "bug," or listening device, in Salerno's Gramercy Park apartment. Salerno had a live-in helper who cooked and did his chores, so getting inside the high-security apartment was a feat in itself. Installing the bug and getting out again undetected was another. The bug was installed and was working properly, but detectives at the listening post (called the "plant") complained that they couldn't make out Fat Tony's conversations. It was Fat Tony's habit to turn on the television set full blast when he entered the apartment with associates, a tactic to muffle conversations in the event there were listening devices around. While the detectives could overhear some of the conversations, the blaring television made it impossible to obtain good recordings for use as evidence. The wiremen devised a way to return to the apartment and rig the television so that it would blow out when it was next turned on.

The plan worked. When Fat Tony's helper next entered the apartment and turned on the TV, it blew. Fat Tony berated him for breaking the television set, but until it was repaired, the detectives received noise-free recordings of the criminal communications in the apartment.

As the gang planned to remodel the Dunhill Barbershop into offices for Merit Commercial, court orders for electronic eavesdropping there were obtained. The bugs were installed at Merit without a hitch, and we began overhearing the inner workings of the world's largest loan-sharking operation. It was big business. The bugs picked up evidence of union racketeers, who, as it turned out, were deeply involved with the Teamsters union.

Nothing moved in the garment district except in trucks, and the Teamsters controlled trucks. Louis Ostrer was Fat Tony's specialist in union plans. Federal investigation of the labor unions made it more difficult for racketeers to drain money out of the unions themselves, so mobsters began looking for new ways to divert union funds. Ostrer was establishing various welfare plans for the Teamsters. He was in debt to the Salerno mob for three-quarters of a million dollars or more. The welfare funds provided ample room for kickbacks from medical suppliers and insurance frauds. In one conversation, Fat Tony's associates revealed that "since the first of the year, this Lou [Ostrer] has put his hands on a million dollars that he got from that insurance." The figures discussed were astronomical.

As the evidence poured in from police surveillance of the Salerno gang's meetings, which were usually called to exchange money, we began to concentrate as well on the activities of Louis Ostrer and others involved with the union plans. The underworld web was tangled, but there was a common link: Anthony "Fat Tony" Salerno. Mob bosses, who were known to the police as powerful crime figures, met Fat Tony outside the Dunhill Barbershop. In Fat Tony's presence, they were submissive and listened and obeyed. The gang hierarchy was well defined and absolute.

We established court-ordered electronic eavesdropping on the premises of Louis Ostrer and others and began gathering evidence about the union welfare plans. It appeared from the evidence that the president of the Teamsters union was to be paid twenty-five thousand dollars for each local union that accepted the plan. One of the search warrants described Louis Ostrer as "a convicted felon whose activities include providing ostensibly legitimate fronts for the investment of illegally obtained monies from organized crime enterprises. . . ."

Salerno gang members were already under indictment from other cases involving their organized criminal gambling and loan-sharking activities. It was time to begin bringing the cases to conclusion. Search warrants were prepared for the premises occupied by Merit Commercial and the Dunhill Barbershop. Racket Squad detectives raided and seized the gang's loan-sharking records. The evidence was overwhelming. Permission was obtained to impanel a special grand jury. It was called the Grand Jury for Special Investigations into Organized Criminal Activities in the County of New York, and that grand jury worked for months reviewing evidence gathered during our investigations. The loan-shark victims did not want to testify. They feared for their lives. Even when confronted with evidence of their conversations with Salerno's gang, it was difficult to get them to admit to borrowing money at usurious rates.

Evidence our detectives overheard justified the loan victims' fear. Salerno directed one of his men to break someone's leg, and the gang conspired to commit murder. The special grand jury indicted many of the loan-shark victims for criminal contempt—a serious felony—for their refusals to testify about their illegal loans. Salerno and many of his associates were indicted for criminal usury and conspiracy.

Search warrants were issued after the long court-ordered electronic surveillance of Louis Ostrer. Ostrer had had conversations in his office with organized crime figures, who had been assured that it was safe to talk there. Ostrer had told the crime figures that he had had his premises "swept,"

The author (left) *with Assistant District Attorney Austin Campriello reviewing loansharking records and evidence seized in the Anthony "Fat Tony" Salerno case*

meaning that they were free of law enforcement bugs. That was clearly not the case, and the Ostrer portion of the investigation produced important evidence of union activities and financial manipulations.

On his arraignment before the supreme court, Salerno's lawyers objected to his being named Anthony "Fat Tony" Salerno in the grand jury's indictment. A lot of mobsters grew up with neighborhood nicknames that stuck with them throughout their lives. Even if the nicknames were not used to their faces, everyone knew Fat Tony, and his arrest, along with the seizure of records of his multimillion-dollar loan-sharking racket, remains one of the law enforcement's major victories against organized crime.

3

DRUGS

Drug addiction is a scourge of modern society. Drug abuse is so prevalent that neither the loss of lives and human productivity nor the economic losses caused by drug addicts committing crimes to pay for their habits can be summed up by statistics alone.

In one year in the United States, ninety-three federal and local law enforcement officers were killed in the line of duty fighting the scourge of drugs. In the last decade, drug arrests in New York City increased 400 percent. Most recent annual statistics log 937,400 drug arrests nationwide.

The United States Drug Enforcement Administration (DEA) reported about ten years ago that its agents seized 2,142.3 kilograms of heroin and cocaine, compared with 55,690.7 kilograms today. These statistics do not count seizures made by local law enforcement groups throughout the United States. In a recent year, statistics showing hospital emergencies related to cocaine amounted to 26,186 cases, compared with 7,054 cocaine-related hospital emergencies the year before. Ten years ago, 184 clandestine drug labs were seized, compared with 810 seized in 1990. Massive increases continue to be reported in the cultivation, production, smuggling, and trafficking of drugs, and in the addiction, hospital cases resulting from drug consumption, and crimes of violence committed by addicts to support their habits, along with accidents and deaths directly related to addicts operating motor vehicles. Drug cartels have held nations at bay, killing antidrug presidential candidates, judges, and justice ministers. In just one month in Colombia, there were 143 drug-related kidnappings.

While there are many drugs of abuse, the principal addictive drugs of choice are heroin, cocaine, marijuana, and pharmaceutical products with stimulant or depressant effects. In all of its forms, drug abuse is deadly. Abusers not only destroy their own lives but often destroy the lives of innocent, unintended victims, family members, and even by-standers, killed in violent street battles among drug dealers.

There are many innocent-sounding street names for drugs. White heroin is called snow; crystallized cocaine is known as crack; PCP is called angel dust; LSD is acid. These fanciful names are for drugs that cause physical and psychological dependence, lingering sickness, or death. While heroin had for some time been the drug of choice for addicts, since 1985 crack has gained widespread use. Mind-altering chemicals like LSD, short for lysergic acid diethylamide, and PCP, or phencyclidine, can be deadly. Prescription drugs with health-promoting medical applications are used by abusers as depressants or stimulants.

As is the case in every area where there is a demand for an illegal product or service, organized criminal gangs move in to supply the demand at big profits, often with elaborate manufacturing, smuggling, and distribution networks. Legitimate businesses such as banks, real estate, and investment firms, and even supermarkets, are taken over by drug traffickers to "launder" money—disguise its source and ownership—enabling criminals to dispose of millions of dollars in small denomination bills, realized from their illicit enterprises.

Background about the nature of some of the major drugs of abuse is helpful to understand the complex problems of drug enforcement and the international criminal syndicate that controls the production and distribution of illicit drugs.

SNOW

Opium addiction has long been a problem in Far Eastern societies, where the poppy flower is cultivated for its sap, which is extracted and refined. Opium that is purified has a medicinal, painkilling use as morphine. Refined opium becomes heroin, an addictive substance that is one drug of choice among abusers.

The poppy flower, *Papaver somniferum*, provides the main source of natural narcotics. Narcotics ease pain, but dangerous side effects can occur even when they are taken under close medical supervision. As addicts seek the pleasure induced by a narcotic, their tolerance to the drug increases, as does their dependence on it. When deprived of the drug, addicts go into physical withdrawal, which can cause symptoms that include tremors, vomiting, chills, pain, and spasms.

As long ago as 300 B.C. the Mediterranean basin was a site for opium poppy cultivation. Afghanistan, Pakistan,

India, and China are prime cultivation sites for the opium poppy today, as is the area of Burma, Laos, and Thailand, which is known as the Golden Triangle. Poppy cultivation in Mexico produces brown Mexican heroin.

The opium poppy is sliced, and the sap that exudes is collected as raw opium. This raw opium is treated with lime and ammonium chloride to reduce it to a morphine base. The reduction of raw opium is an important step for traffickers because it decreases the weight of the product to be transported. The morphine base weighs only one-tenth of the original opium sap, enabling smugglers to carry it overland.

New processes now make it possible to extract the chemicals of opium from the mature, dried poppy plant, called poppy straw, and this has modernized the opium collection process. These chemical alkaloids of opium also form the basis for today's legal narcotic manufacture. Morphine products are used in painkillers and cough medicine, as relaxants for intestinal problems, and to relieve diarrhea.

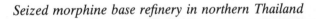

Seized morphine base refinery in northern Thailand

Heroin is synthesized from morphine. Pure white Asian heroin is refined in the Golden Triangle, although heroin can appear in many colors, from off-white to brown. The color results from impurities introduced in the manufacturing process or from substances used to dilute the heroin, which can include brown sugar, cocoa, and food coloring. It was pure Asian heroin smuggled to France, then into the United States by organized crime figures, that became the focus of the famous "French Connection" case in New York City.

When illicit heroin reaches the street market and is sold to drug addicts in "bags," the purity has been greatly reduced. Heroin is "cut," or diluted many times, so that the street bag, sometimes called the nickel bag, only contains 5 percent heroin in a hundred-milligram bulk, having been mixed and diluted with powdered milk, sugar, starch, and even quinine. Crude Mexican heroin appears on the street in the form of black tar. This sticky substance is sold in higher percentages of purity, then diluted with other substances so that it can be injected after being dissolved by heating.

Opium trafficking in the Golden Triangle, a spur of sparsely populated jungle land, is controlled by hill tribes and by an organized paramilitary regime called the Shan State Armies. These armies are highly trained and well equipped with the latest antiaircraft and antipersonnel weapons. In Burma's Shan State, there is little or no government control; the organized paramilitary forces have thousands of troops, and it is here that more than 75 percent of all Golden Triangle opium is produced. Warlords reign supreme in the Shan States. Farmers who produce and harvest the crop are taxed by the Shan lords and often are impressed into their armies.

In the countries of the Golden Triangle, profits from heroin smuggling are used to pay off government, military, and police officials at the highest levels. During the Vietnam War, United States intelligence groups encouraged and eased this heroin trafficking—or looked the other way—to insure the uninterrupted operation of United States military activities.

The narcotics trade in the Golden Triangle is quite organized. Farmers deal with a series of middlemen—drug merchants like the Yunnanese Chinese—who pay low prices for the raw opium, then sell it to other traders or form huge caravans and mule trains to transport it under the protection of the private armies to crude refining plants in the jungle.

Once processed, usually in the border areas in the north of Thailand near Burma, the opium gum or morphine base is shipped farther south, usually by pack trains, into Thailand. There, highly sophisticated refineries, built in the jungles, further refine and reduce the bulk of the opium or opium extracts.

Once refined, the pure white Golden Triangle heroin is smuggled from Thailand, a nation with a population of more than half a million heroin addicts. The heroin enters Burma and then goes south through Malaysia to Hong Kong and through Hawaii into the mainstream United States markets. My investigations revealed widespread trafficking networks in Thailand and Vietnam during the Vietnam War. Some dealers even transported heroin concealed in the bodies of American servicemen killed in action.

On the street, the effects of narcotics abuse are evident. Gang violence among traffickers has resulted in open warfare. Murders are committed using sophisticated automatic weapons, and bloody duels are fought among organized criminal gangs vying for millions in profit from illegal drug traffic. Deaths by overdose, ruined lives, and diseases spread to users and their sexual partners from unsanitary drug paraphernalia are everywhere creating havoc in modern society.

Detectives from a police department specialized squad joined forces with the Racket Squad to investigate the growth of organized drug trafficking. Warrants were issued, and when the evidence was studied, it became eminently clear why drug selling was on the rise. Account books seized by the detectives showed huge profits by middle-level drug wholesalers. They sold heroin and cocaine to pushers, who in turn cut the drugs' purity and sold them to street sellers. The network was clearly defined, but it was so vast and the profits so great that for every drug seller arrested, it seemed as if a hundred more sprang up to take his place.

Every initiative taken by the police to curtail drug trafficking seemed doomed to failure. In one situation, an assistant district attorney from our office who was assigned to court asked me to appear for him because he had another appointment.

"It's a junk collar," the assistant DA said. "Just take a felony plea and recommend a year in jail with credit for time served," he told me. I picked up the file and looked for the defendant's criminal record. This "yellow sheet" showed the record of arrests and convictions. The guy had three pages of criminal arrests. He was a professional drug seller. But in the world of criminal courts, plea bargaining is an everyday occurrence. Defendants who plead guilty are permitted to plead guilty to lesser offenses and given assurance of easy sentences, with very little jail time. If every defendant pleaded not guilty and every case had to be tried, it's reasoned, the court system would collapse.

When the case was called, the criminal drug seller ap-

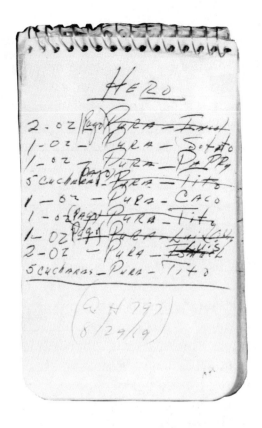

Prices of pure heroin (marked PURA) in *midlevel drug wholesaler's notebook, with names of his dealers and quantities sold. Those crossed out mean the dealers paid for their drugs (marked PAGO).*

peared from the pen, the court's jail holding facility, between two armed court officers. The defendant was carrying a pile of papers. The judge looked down from the bench and asked what the People intended to do with the case. "Your Honor, the People, on the recommendation of the assistant district attorney assigned to the case, are prepared to recommend the acceptance of a plea to . . ." I announced the recommended jail sentence of one year. Before I was even able to get the complete statement out, the defendant threw his sheaf of papers down on the counsel table and shouted to the court, "No, man. I ain't gonna take that. My friend pleaded out and got seven month. I ain't gonna take nothin' more than seven month."

43

"The plea offer is withdrawn. . . ." The defendant was taken back into the pens as his lawyer whispered in his ear. The sad truth is that when that case came up on the next court date, this professional drug seller, whose only business was selling drugs, and who was arrested for the sale of heroin to two different undercover police officers, would surely get his "seven month." With credit for time served, in jail awaiting trial or disposition of his case, the pusher would walk out of the courtroom that very day and within a few hours be back on the street selling heroin.

In the end, the courts are defeating their own purpose. Strangled by the sheer volume of cases, courts and prosecutors try to reduce their caseloads by plea bargaining arrangements that put criminals on the streets to commit more crimes. This is called revolving-door justice. The volume is further increased every time professional drug sellers are let off with light or inconsequential sentences. Pushers go back to selling drugs until they are arrested again.

Some of the classic racketeering gangs entered the lucrative drug trade; others did not, keeping their businesses "clean" of junk, sticking to numbers, gambling, loan-sharking, union racketeering, and infiltration of ostensibly legitimate businesses. The gangs that entered the heroin-trafficking racket served as importers, easing heroin smuggling from major European centers like Paris, Amsterdam, London, Rome, Milan, and Brussels. When pressure was applied by drug enforcement officials, racketeers used their influence with corrupt police officers to foil detection and arrest.

As heroin traffic blossomed, new routes into the United States and Europe were sought. Heroin from Turkey, Afghanistan, and Lebanon flooded the marketplaces as drug agents concentrated on Asian heroin-trafficking routes. As more attention was placed on Middle East heroin trafficking, supplies from Mexico began making their appearances in the United States. Organized criminal gangs establish drug-trafficking networks throughout the world to cash in on this lucrative racket.

COCAINE

High in the Andes, leaves of the coca plant, *Erythroxylon coca*, have been chewed since prehistoric times. The extract from these leaves is made into cocaine, which has medical applications as an anesthetic that limits bleeding by constricting blood vessels. Illicit use of cocaine as a stimulant has gained in popularity among drug abusers because of its abundance and the ease of using cocaine hydrochloride, the white powder injected, snorted, or smoked by abusers. Chunks or rocks of cocaine derivative are called "crack." The cocaine base substance in its "rock," or "crack," form is vaporized in a cigarette, or "joint," or smoked in a pipe. Breathing the fumes deeply into their lungs, addicts derive an immediate high from crack, but the high wears off quickly, making abusers need repeated doses.

Of United States Drug Enforcement Administration arrests in one recent year alone, 60 percent of the offenses involved cocaine. In that year, the DEA arrests, not counting additional arrests from local law enforcement agencies in the United States, amounted to 14,116 for cocaine, 2,403 for heroin, 4,170 for marijuana, and 3,283 for other dangerous drugs. The increase in cocaine and crack abuse has led to hospital emergency wards overflowing with victims suffering overdose symptoms: heart failure, cerebral hemorrhage, lung and respiratory failure, and toxic shock.

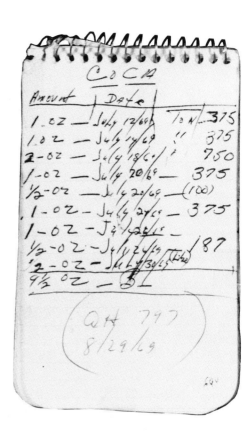

*Cocaine sales listed
with prices paid in a
drug dealer's notebook*

In Latin America, where the coca plants are harvested and cocaine is refined for transport to the United States, wars have raged openly between government forces and cartels. Fortunes from the illicit traffic have provided the cartels with armies of hoodlums and the power to corrupt whole governments. Coca leaves come from Peru, Bolivia, Colombia, and Ecuador. DEA statistics about coca production show an enormous increase in only five years: Gross cultivation in Peru, the primary source of coca leaves, amounted to 120,170 hectares compared to 95,200 five years before. In that year 9,000 hectares of coca leaf cultivation were eradicated compared to 4,830 five years earlier.

The DEA reports that Bolivia is the primary source for cocaine base and paste. The cocaine base is transported to Colombia, a primary source for cocaine hydrochloride and a distribution point for cocaine. It requires about five hundred kilograms of dry coca leaves to yield one kilogram of cocaine hydrochloride. DEA authorities estimate 100 to 130 metric tons of cocaine hydrochloride are produced annually. In one year alone, DEA agents seized some ten metric tons of cocaine. The DEA estimates that cocaine has a street value in the United States of from $10,000 to $37,500 per kilogram. It is easy to see how billions of dollars are realized each year from illicit cocaine traffic. It is to the drug trafficker's advantage to increase consumption of cocaine, especially among America's school children and young adults. This population of young people are most susceptible to taking chances with drug abuse. Most young people think

Baskets of coca leaves

that they are too strong willed and physically fit to get "hooked." No one is powerful enough to come through drug abuse unscathed, and the harm often scars a person for life.

"There's no such thing as a former addict," the Racket Squad detective in charge of narcotics said. "I've never really seen a reformed addict. Sometimes they get over it for a while, but the weakness, the psychological craving, is always there. I've been at this for twenty-five years, and believe me, I've seen everything. Once hooked on drugs, the rest is just waiting for the eventual end to come," the detective said. The echo of the veteran detective's words, his very pessimistic view of drug rehabilitation and treatment programs, may not be too far from the sad truth. Many persons in law enforcement and in drug rehabilitation programs share, perhaps not in intensity but in persuasion, the opinion of this Racket Squad detective.

CANNABIS

Cannabis sativa, the hemp plant, is a weed. It grows well almost anywhere and thrives in tropical climates. Concentrated in its leaves and flowering tops is a powerful drug that has been used throughout the centuries in a number of forms. Marijuana, formed into a tobacco by drying the leaves, which concentrate the chemical, provides psychoactive highs to users who smoke the "joints." Hashish is made from secretions of the cannabis plant, as is hashish oil. The production and smuggling of cannabis into the United States by organized criminals has netted them billions of dollars. The drug is funneled into the mainstream by racketeering fronts—everything from fishing fleets to lumber companies—operated as ostensibly legitimate businesses.

HALLUCINOGENS AND PRESCRIPTION DRUGS

Reporters from the *Daily News*, a major New York City newspaper, received an anonymous tip about the number of bogus prescriptions being filled by pharmacies for amphetamines and barbiturates. The newspaper brought the case to the Rackets Bureau, and we began an investigation with the help of the New York State Pharmaceutical Society.

One of the reporters, working undercover, had a messenger deliver an order for prescription forms to a printer in the name of D. M. Sugob (Bogus M.D. spelled backward). The phony doctor's address on the prescription pads was for the Federation Against Drug Addiction. A control telephone number was put on the prescription pads to track any calls pharmacists might make to the doctor. Five dangerous

Assistant District Attorney John C. Fine with Chief Assistant District Attorney Alfred J. Scotti reviewing description of controlled substances during the pharmacy investigation

drugs popular with drug abusers were chosen for this investigation. Any of the drugs should have alerted a vigilant pharmacist. No federal narcotics registry number was supplied on the prescription blanks.

The printer of the forms was chosen at random from the yellow pages. The first printer refused the order. The second supplied the printed prescription blanks in the name of Dr. Sugob at a cost of $13.38 for one thousand forms, no questions asked.

A reporter filled out the prescription blanks, using pharmaceutical terminology and symbols found in any dictionary. The drugs ordered were Bamadex, an amphetamine used for weight reduction, which when improperly used serves as an "upper"; Desbutal, another weight control substance, which the manufacturers say must be used with "extreme caution," and a well-known "upper"; Benzedrine, a weight-control drug notorious on the illicit drug market; Nembutal, which produces drowsiness and is considered a "downer" among drug abusers; and Seconal Sodium, another habit-forming hypnotic sedative, also a "downer."

Five *Daily News* reporters were given five prescriptions each. They fanned out around New York City to have them filled. Every reporter returned with drugs. Out of sixty-two pharmacies visited by the reporters, a total of sixteen prescriptions were filled. Thirty-two pharmacies said they were out of the drug requested, and only fourteen pharmacies asked for the federal narcotics registry number missing from the prescription blanks. An obvious error was made in the prescription for Bamadex. The instructions stated that it be taken by the patient before bedtime. Bamadex is a powerful stimulant and the manufacturer recommends that it be taken in the morning. Four of the five Bamadex prescriptions were filled. One pharmacist marked the label "One capsule as directed," telling the reporter-customer to check with his doctor. Two other pharmacists caught the error but filled the prescription. The fourth pharmacist made no mention at all about the obvious error.

The investigation proved how easy it is to obtain powerful and dangerous drugs through bogus prescriptions. It was also clear from further investigations that some doctors made their living by supplying illicit drugs to abusers. Many wrote prescriptions for profits; others dispensed drugs without any valid medical need to addicts and drug abusers with money to pay.

Hallucinogens are chemical substances, consisting of everything from peyote and mescaline derived from the peyote cactus used by Mexican Indians from earliest times in religious ceremonies to substances distilled from mushrooms like the *Psilocybe*. This "sacred" mushroom, which is a mood-altering drug similar to LSD, is a substance found naturally in morning glory seeds. All of these mind-altering drugs, including phencyclidine, or PCP ("angel dust"), often create uncontrollable psychic reactions that cause various forms of insanity. Many deaths are associated with irrational actions by those under the influence of hallucinogens.

In New York City alone, drug arrests jumped from 18,113 to 89,112 in only nine years. The numbers are alarming, as these statistics represent the worldwide trend of increasing use and availability of narcotics, profitably smuggled into countries by an underworld of organized criminals.

Drug trafficking is organized. But as some of the cases cited have shown, society is not organized to prevent it. "Snow" and "angel dust" are just euphemisms. These substances have been corrupted for a human pleasure that can destroy life itself.

4

ELECTRONIC SPIES

Surreptitious spying in today's technological world is easy, effective, and illegal. Wiretapping (illegally intercepting telephone communications) and bugging (secretly listening in to conversations) is a "dirty business," as Supreme Court Justice Oliver Wendell Holmes put it many years ago. When illegally overheard private communications are used to gain business advantage, as is done in commercial espionage cases, or for blackmail and extortion, or to destroy a person's privacy or right to free expression, it is not only a dirty business, it is an abuse of advanced technology for the commission of serious crime.

In the United States the right to privacy is secured by the Constitution, and protected by state and federal laws that make invasion of privacy a serious crime. If law enforcement officials want to legally intercept telephone conversations or listen secretly to personal communications without the permission of at least one party, they must obtain a court-ordered warrant. With the widespread use of inexpensive audio and video electronic equipment, everyone and anyone can tap a phone or bug a private conversation. Equipment for that purpose is for sale in any drug or electronics store that sells portable tape recorders or video equipment.

Gangsters have long evaded law enforcement probes by hiring electronic eavesdropping experts to sweep their offices and homes for law enforcement's bugs and wiretaps, and they themselves have engaged in illegal wiretapping and eavesdropping to commit various crimes, including elaborate schemes to cheat bookmakers and betting offices operated by rival gangs.

Using the tools of espionage, made easy today by advanced technology, illegal electronic surveillance is one of the most prevalent crimes committed by gangsters and ruthless business competitors. How it's done and what's being done to stop it is one of the least discussed law enforcement topics today.

THE INVESTIGATIONS

Manny Mittleman was an electronic wizard who operated his electronic eavesdropping business on Liberty Street in lower Manhattan under the name Wireless Guitar Company. Mittleman was considered the best. In the business many years, Manny covered himself by offering his services to law enforcement officials seeking out sophisticated electronic interception devices, but he also built devices for anyone he thought could be trusted.

A businessman presented himself in the DA's office complaining that his former partner, now an arch business rival, was obtaining leads for contacting customers that he could

53

only have learned by using unlawful means. Suspecting that this businessman's private communications were being intercepted, we dispatched "wiremen," police detectives assigned to the Racket Squad who have training and expertise in electronic surveillance. Our squad's wiremen were reputed to be the best police electronic surveillance experts in the world. These specialized detectives also installed legal electronic intercepts under court order.

Our wiremen discovered the victim's telephone had been tapped and that conversations were being recorded in the basement of the building. The detectives established a stakeout and found that a private detective had conducted the illegal surveillance. As we listened to the tape with the victim, it was clear that his business rival was behind the espionage. Posing as a messenger for the private detective, an assistant district attorney telephoned the suspected business rival. When he was told that there was "some good stuff on the tape," the rival took the bait.

A rendezvous was set up so that the person behind the illegal interception could pick up the most recent tape recordings. As the men prepared to part, the business rival asked the undercover detective if there was anything else.

"Oh, yes, one thing . . .," the detective answered. As the man turned to hear what he thought would be more intelligence, the detective produced his shield and placed him under arrest. The criminal was apprehended in front of thousands of New York City pedestrians and put in a large Cadillac, a vehicle the officer frequently used under cover. "Show me your photo ID again. I don't believe you're a cop," the arrested man exclaimed. The private detective who had conducted the espionage was also apprehended.

Identification of equipment used in this and in a number

of unsolved eavesdropping cases led our expert wiremen to suggest that Manny Mittleman had made the wiretapping device. District Attorney Hogan's chief investigator, Tom Fay, was in charge of a small squad of men on the "tightrope," a special kind of undercover work. These men infiltrated corrupt trade unions and racketeering activities, especially those areas that involved official corruption. They were able to work under cover on police or government officials' corruption cases without being identified. Their work was dangerous. These men often entered situations alone, unarmed, sometimes without a "wire" that would enable them to summon help. This was to prevent detection if they were searched.

Tom Fay assigned his best men. Strategy was mapped out to identify the major sellers of illegal eavesdropping equipment as well as those who manufactured it.

Gerry Edwards, an investigator with expert senses of observation and recall, became our principal undercover operative. Gerry was shorter than the minimum height requirement for police officers, looked nothing like a law

Mittleman's famed wireless bug. This small transmitter, powered by a battery, could send a clear conversation to eavesdroppers waiting nearby.

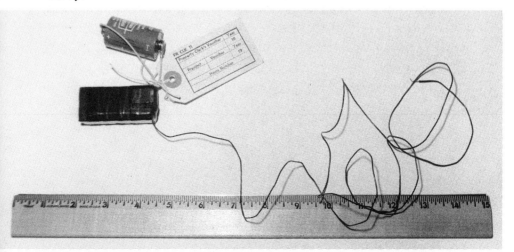

enforcement agent, and his skill and ability enabled him to penetrate activities associated with organized crime when other detectives failed. We began by targeting people our wiremen suspected as sellers of illicit eavesdropping equipment. Some of these criminal wiretappers had known associations with organized crime figures. Working under cover, Investigator Edwards equipped himself with his own concealed microphone, one so small that detection would be unlikely, even by the most suspicious spy.

Edwards offered to buy eavesdropping equipment, then allowed Mittleman and other suspects to talk, establishing the criminal intent required by law to convict them.

Manny Mittleman was coy. Years of experience dealing with both law enforcement officials and spies made him cautious, suspicious of everyone. Investigator Edwards was able to make important observations inside Mittleman's Wireless Guitar Company, observations that, coupled with his report and recorded conversations, enabled the DA's office to obtain a search warrant. On the day of the "buy," Edwards entered Mittleman's premises as backup detectives stood by, waiting for the signal. Inspector Paul Vitrano had mobilized the Racket Squad. Detectives fanned out around the city, standing by at other locations that Edwards's investigations had turned up. Once one raid was made, the others had to follow immediately. If word got out, the sellers would dump the goods and the search teams would come up empty-handed. The detectives, wiremen, and specialized investigative accountants, who would review business records and documents that could incriminate customers of the illegal equipment, awaited the signal that would trigger the raids.

Mittleman was proud of his work, now effusive in his comments about its use. Investigator Edwards obtained his

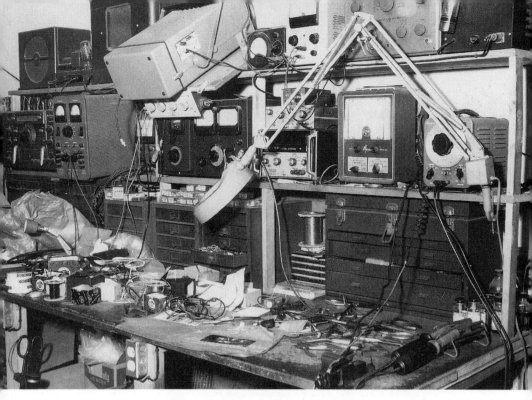

Electronic eavesdropping workshop raided by Racket Squad detectives

eavesdropping device, signaled his backup team, and the officers executed the search warrant, taking the king of surreptitious spies into custody.

Eavesdroppers and makers of eavesdropping equipment were quickly rounded up around the city. The search warrants netted hundreds of wiretapping devices, sophisticated telephone intercept instruments, room bugs, remote-controlled wireless transmitters, mini drop-in transmitters, and an assortment of secret spying equipment.

The wiremen studied the equipment seized in the raids and compared it to devices their own investigations and telephone company security men had been turning up. It was clear that we had brought to justice people who had been responsible for manufacturing and distributing equipment used in illicit eavesdropping operations around the world.

57

*Warehouse of electronic eavesdropping devices raided by
Racket Squad detectives*

"No question about it, that's Manny's stuff," one of the
wiremen said, examining a room bug so small that it could
be easily concealed in a wall receptacle or inside the body
of a telephone. Manny's trademark was a black epoxy resin
he used to conceal his inventions once the little devices were
crammed with tiny electronic components. As small as the
devices were, they could broadcast over fairly long distances
using FM radio bands.

"But you prove it in court," the wireman added, smiling
as he continued to examine the evidence.

Manny Mittleman took the stand to testify in his own
behalf. The acknowledged dean of electronic eavesdropping
wizards refused to answer questions about one of his ultra-
sophisticated inventions, a harmonica bug. His refusal was

coupled with a knowing, furtive smile and twinkle in his eyes—pride for having his invention recognized in court. Pride in authorship or not, Mittleman was convicted and sent to jail, putting an end to the infamous Wireless Guitar Company.

THE HARDWARE

The eavesdropping equipment seized by the squad ranged from simple induction coils attached to a rubber suction cup that enabled tape recording of a telephone conversation, to Mittleman's harmonica bugs, activated when the eavesdropper blew a note on a harmonica. The tone-operated devices would enable a spy in Los Angeles to eavesdrop on a conversation in Miami or anyplace else in the world. The detectives uncovered electronic equipment used by underworld gamblers, even devices that enabled observers at race tracks to communicate winning horses to accomplices at bookmaking parlors before bets were closed on the race.

"That's a stinger," one of the detectives explained, demonstrating how two silver dimes connected to a remote-controlled radio signaling device could be used by professional card cheats. "The player would tape the dimes like electrodes to his stomach. The dimes were wired to a small radio-wave receiver concealed in the harness. An accomplice would position herself (it was frequently a good-looking woman) so that she could see the other players' hands. With a concealed transmitter, the accomplice would telegraph signals to the player, who received electric shocks, telling him the cards," the detective continued. "This is a pretty crude device. You can imagine the pain as the electrodes emitted shocks on the player's skin, stinging him as many times as it took each night to rake in a bundle. I guess the money they made was worth the pain. But a little electrocution wouldn't be all they'd get if the mob found out they were cheating on one of their racket-controlled gaming operations," the detective added seriously, knowing of cases where the stinger ended up dead, the victim of mob violence.

One of the most frequently used telephone tapping devices unearthed by the detectives was a starter device. The starter is used once the eavesdropper has located a particular telephone line. Each telephone wire comes into a building on a line or set of lines. Most have four wires, but only two of them typically are used for the telephone. The line goes from the house, apartment, or commercial premises to a junction box, a place where the telephone company has brought many telephone customers' lines together. The junction box in an apartment house or office building is often in a utility closet. The local junction box is connected by a trunk line to the building's main junction box, often in the basement of the building, sometimes outside on a pole or somewhere on the street. Private dwellings have separate wires that run along telephone poles to remote junction boxes. Even a casual observer will remember seeing a telephone lineman with something like a telephone handset dangling from his belt, climbing a pole, working at a junction box. The local junction box takes the telephone wires to a telephone company switching station for the district.

The wiretapper first identifies the particular wires of the phone line targeted for illegal interception. That can be done by gaining access to any junction box and listening in until the targeted voice, business, or number is located. Frequently the eavesdropper simply gains access to the premises and attaches a buzzer to the phone lines inside. The criminal eavesdropper then takes the lineman's handset, which is simply another telephone that can clip onto the junction box where the wires are attached. He runs the two clips down the junction box wires until he hears the buzzing sound made by the battery-operated noise emitter attached to the victim's telephone line. This can be done at the local junction box or at a point farther away. For the wiretapper, this is the riskiest part of the business; it is where stealth and burglary are committed.

Law enforcement officials can get the identification of lines for a particular number from the telephone company with a court-authorized warrant. This simplifies the process of choosing the proper location for a telephone tap.

Once the lines are identified, the criminal eavesdropper need only attach the starter to the junction box, or splice it into the telephone wires themselves, attach a tape recorder, and the starter will activate the tape recorder automatically when there is action on the line, much like an answering machine. There will be no indication to callers that anyone is listening in. Since the tape recorder is activated only when someone is on the line, tape is conserved and the eavesdropper can collect the tapes at the least dangerous times.

An even safer method criminals use to tap telephones is called "stealing a spare." There are more telephone lines in buildings than there are customers. This permits the telephone company to add phones if there is additional demand without stringing extra wires or rewiring. Unused telephone lines in a building are called spares. If a set of live wires is spliced into a set of spares in a junction box, then the unused phone wires can be picked up at a remote relay point, in effect giving the wiretapper another extension on the victim's phone line. The criminal can receive the victim's calls over existing phone company equipment at some concealed, safe location. Often wiretappers rent offices, put in call-forwarding equipment, and then never show up anywhere near the original connections to intercept calls or collect tapes. Stealing a spare minimizes the amount of equipment that has to be left in the area of a junction box. Sophisticated wiretappers do their work carefully so that there is no telltale wiring that could be easily detected by phone company employees doing routine repairs. The only connection made in the premise's junction box or on the phone lines is a subtle splice from the victim's phone lines to a set of spares.

Hidden microphones that pick up conversations, then transmit them over the airwaves to a remote location where the eavesdropper has established a listening post, offer secrecy and versatility that wire-connected microphones do not. Room bugs, like telephone taps, require electrical power. Telephone taps are parasitic—they use the phone company's power supply. Some room bugs, those hidden in telephone or electrical appliances or wall outlets, are also parasitic, using the wiring in the building. Some room bugs are powered by stringing wires, running the wires to a telephone junction box or to some other location directly. These wires are often difficult to install and require break-ins. There is the ever-present risk of detection as alien wiring is discovered and traced to the plant.

Wireless transmitters using FM bands or, in some cases, private radio bands, give the criminal wiretapper flexibility. A simple FM transmitter is the drop-in. Drop-ins are nothing more than a microphone and radio transmitter made to look like the carbon mike in any telephone mouthpiece.

The telephone mouthpiece is unscrewed, the counterfeit

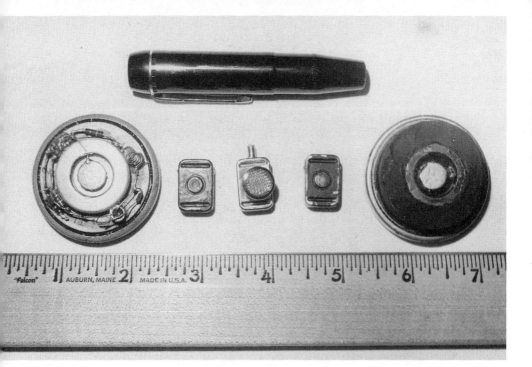

Drop-in transmitter (far left) *before the epoxy is poured to conceal the electronic components. The drop-in transmitter is ready to be placed in any telephone mouthpiece* (far right). *Once installed, it serves as a wireless microphone transmitting the conversation over FM radio frequencies. Also pictured are miniature microphones for spying and a microphone concealed in a pen.*

carbon mike is "dropped in," and when the plastic mouthpiece cover is screwed back, the device broadcasts telephone conversations as well as any conversation in the room. Drop-ins usually have a short range, generally not more than a couple of blocks, and transmit signals over the FM radio band. The danger with these devices, and others that broadcast over FM or television bands, is their interference with regular radio and television programming in the neighborhood. One big case was broken when a neighbor complained that his favorite program was being interrupted by amorous conversations from the apartment next door.

With its ready source of power, a variety of bugs can be

hooked into the telephone instrument or on its wiring. Room bugs used in conjunction with telephones tap the phone as well as conversations near the instrument. The simplest room bug looks like a black square the size of a sugar cube and can be hooked inside the telephone. This device converts the phone mouthpiece into an open microphone, usually more sophisticated and effective than the drop-in transmitter. The room bug may be in the telephone company's wall jack, and some are even prefabricated to look like official telephone company property. Others resemble electric sockets placed behind the wall plate. Many bugs have powerful batteries and the miniaturized circuitry of space-age technology.

Manny Mittleman's invention, the harmonica bug, or any one of the tone-activated bugs in use today, depends on a sound for activation. When it is installed in a telephone, it enables a caller to phone the victim's number from anyplace in the world. A tone blown on a harmonica or a touch-tone beep activates the bug even before the phone rings in the victim's premises. The same principle is used in sophisticated phone answering machines, where a touch-tone telephone is used to signal the machine on the other end to do something. The harmonica bug or a telephone touch-tone–activated bug costs about $3,500 on the illicit marketplace.

A bug can be in a briefcase, activated before a business executive leaves the room. He can then listen in on a radio receiver as the conversation continues in his absence. Bugs can be used by politicians who spy on their rivals. Employers in and out of government spy on their employees using audio devices and concealed cameras. Foreign agents secretly obtain information for intelligence purposes or in order to blackmail a victim into betraying a trust for espionage. Totalitarian governments spy on citizens to maintain power. All of these are ways in which electronic surveillance and sophisticated eavesdropping technology have been used to invade privacy.

Gangsters use high-tech equipment to spy on others and to sweep their own premises to detect law enforcement taps and bugs. Some have even employed the services of eavesdroppers to corrupt public officials or persons whose indiscretions make them susceptible to extortion. People who have frequented bars and gambling casinos owned by crime figures can be set up and lured into compromising situations that are clandestinely videotaped and recorded. Mobsters have even used electronic eavesdropping to check on the loyalty of members of their own gang.

Electronic eavesdropping is an effective law enforcement tool for obtaining evidence of secret criminal conspiracies, but it must be used under strict safeguards and court supervision to protect individual liberties. Eavesdropping *is* "a dirty business," and it is so easy with modern technology that law enforcement vigilance, in spite of other priorities, must devote resources to apprehending and prosecuting those who would violate the law.

5

COUNTERFEITS

Trademarks are symbols, designs, distinctive words, slogans, or even sounds that identify a maker's goods or services. When a trademark is used to identify a service, it is called a service mark. Trademarks are the words or designs that appear on the package or on the product itself—a brand name or logo. Service marks often appear in advertisements for the product to identify the services offered. Trademarks and service marks in the United States are registered with the Department of Commerce Patent and Trademark Office. Copyrights differ from trademarks because they are designed to protect artistic compositions or literary works. Copyrights are registered with the Library of Congress Copyright Office in the United States. While there may be some overlapping, the essence of trademark protection is that it insures the integrity of a symbol or series of symbols that represent a maker's good name and reputation. Patents, registered with another division of the same office in the Department of Commerce, protect inventions. Most nations of the world have a system for trademark, copyright, and patent registration, with reciprocal arrangements for filing foreign registrations.

Consumers rely on the quality of brand names. People often pay more for specific products they know are backed by a maker's good name and reputation. Hallmarks are established to denote the quality of an item being sold. Gold is stamped with a hallmark to denote fineness and purity. Twenty-four-karat gold, stamped 24K, is pure, or 100 percent, gold. Twenty-four-karat gold is too soft to be used in jewelry, so it is alloyed, or mixed, with silver, nickel, or copper. Fourteen-karat gold is made of fourteen parts gold and ten parts of the alloy metal; eighteen-karat gold is made up of eighteen parts gold and six parts of the alloy. Gold is stamped 24K, 18K, or 14K. The more alloyed the gold, the lesser its purity and value.

Carat spelled with a *c* is used to denote the weight of precious stones. A one-carat diamond weighs a fifth of a gram. It requires 142 one-carat diamonds to weigh an ounce. Silver is also marked for fineness, with most American-made sterling silver containing 925 parts of silver, 1000 denoting pure silver.

In all of this there is ample opportunity for criminals to counterfeit trademarks, logos, and packaging, even to produce cheap imitation jewelry, selling it to unsuspecting shoppers or to bargain hunters. Some buyers of counterfeit brands are fooled by their own greed, hoping to scoop up a Rolex, Piaget, or Omega watch at a cheap price, because they suspect it is "hot," or stolen.

The ease with which products and labels can be counterfeited, then distributed and sold with relatively little risk of getting caught or jailed, has made counterfeiting trademarks and copyrighted labels, as well as false hallmark stamping, a lucrative trade of organized crime.

FRAGRANT FRAUDS

It smelled something like Vitalis hair lotion in an Airwick base—not altogether disagreeable, vaguely reminiscent of the disinfectant odor of a public rest room. At ten dollars a bottle, the marks thought they were buying Chanel perfume. The packaging was an excellent copy of the real thing, and most consumers assumed they were getting genuine French perfume, stolen and being fenced cheap. What the buyers were getting was stung—in a clever underworld con that takes in thousands of people every year.

These fragrant frauds are usually hawked on street corners, at flea markets, and from sidewalk stands, although there have been many cases where the counterfeit item has turned up in discount stores. Without exception, every holiday season is heralded with a spate of fraudulent perfumes. The counterfeits almost perfectly imitate the bottles and outside packaging of Guerlain and Chanel, with all the fancy wrappings of fragrances that can cost $120 per ounce or more. Chemically imitating fragrances is relatively simple and by and large legal, as long as the scent imitators do not use the copied perfume's trademark. Racketeers who manufacture, package, and sell sleazy imitations do little more than run artificial coloring into cheap scents, including hair tonics, add rubbing alcohol, and package the perfume with counterfeit labels.

Our police raids on a counterfeit perfume maker yielded sealing wax, stampers, printed cartons, empty bottles, and assorted packaging materials, along with gallons of the odorous concoctions. The success of this and other consumer frauds described here have a common thread. Those who hope to find bargains that are too good to be true because they assume the items were stolen are victims of their own cunning.

COMMON CLOTH

What do Pierre Cardin and Emilio Gucci have in common with Levi Strauss? Perhaps very little except a good name that's become something of a household word. Makers pay handsomely for the instant recognition of their trademarks and logos, symbols of status and indications of quality.

Millions of dollars' worth of advertising and publicity are poured into the development of trade names and service marks, and manufacturers like Pierre Cardin and Emilio Gucci have served notice that they are not about to permit violations of trademark and copyright laws simply because law enforcement officials, worldwide, ignore counterfeiters, whose cheap imitations and inferior products are stamped Cardin, Gucci, or Levi's.

While it may be the ultimate compliment to copy an artist's style, Italian luggage maker Emilio Gucci has taken his battle to the streets, where Romans have been buying up Gucci handbags for a lot fewer lira than they pay in fashionable showrooms. The fraudulent counterfeits have found their way across the ocean, and fake Gucci bags turn up in great quantities in the United States as well as in Europe and the Far East. Gucci himself is fuming mad. Picture it: a whole nation carrying around little *G*'s. Even

Counterfeit Levi's jeans patches

a draft horse on the Via Veneto can eat his oats out of a Gucci bag.

While it is easy to make light of the problem, the crime that might only seem funny to some has become a billion-dollar-a-year rip-off scam. It is so lucrative that gangsters involved in organized crime have taken over the counterfeiting racket. To the criminal mind, counterfeiting brand names and packaging beats the potential of severe sentences that can be imposed for counterfeiting currency, and it is certainly a lot easier.

Counterfeiters are so organized that even distinctive buttons, pocket patches, and clipped-on guarantee cards, such as those on genuine Levi's jeans, look genuine.

HIS MASTER'S VOICE

The proprietor of a small recording company, specializing in Latin music, presented himself in the Racket Squad offices with two record albums that seemed identical. One was the genuine article, manufactured by his company; the other was an almost perfect counterfeit, right down to the label on the plastic disc. The company official was distraught. His business was being ruined by the counterfeits, and his company was small enough to immediately feel the economic impact.

Counterfeit labels of major recording hits

*Racket Squad detective Adolfo Bermudez seizing counterfeit
phonograph records*

A detective assigned from the squad began picking up
the thread of the investigation on the street, where the counterfeit record was bought. The detective went from record
store to record store, first posing as a buyer, obtaining copies
of the illicit discs, then, as the investigation progressed,
working under cover as a seller of counterfeit records
himself.

The investigation was painstaking. We worked back from
street seller and store owner to the counterfeit record dis-
tributor, then the source of the supply. Based on the sale of
counterfeit records to the undercover detective, we executed
search warrants, taking record store owners into custody,
charging them with New York penal law and business law
violations. Eventually witnesses gave us the names of their
suppliers. Surveillances and the use of informers resulted in

the identification of a phonograph record manufacturing plant in Queens, New York. After obtaining a search warrant, we mobilized the Racket Squad in a raid on the illegal operation.

A search of the plant revealed thousands of counterfeit albums and labels along with newly pressed records. Thousands of counterfeit RCA Victor *Sound of Music* albums were in cartons, awaiting shipment and distribution. Counterfeit labels for many major hits were uncovered by the detectives, who also seized the record presses and wrapping equipment. The machinery seized at this one small record-pressing company was capable of turning out thousands of

One Racket Squad detective searches for bootleg records while another interrogates suspects in a record counterfeiting factory raided by police.

counterfeit phonograph records a day. The bandit's cost was less than twenty-five cents a record. The Recording Industry Association of America, which engaged a special counsel and a task force to combat record and tape piracy, estimated a yearly loss of about $250 million in revenues to legitimate manufacturers.

Counterfeiting, or pirating, records and tapes is easy. Counterfeiters buy an original album or tape. They find a printer who asks no questions, or in some cases, they set up their own photo-offset printing presses. It is virtually the same process used to make copies while you wait in photocopy stores. A picture is taken of the original label, tape, or album cover, complete with anticounterfeiting protection notices, and offset printing plates are made. The counterfeiters take the original album or tape to a studio that specializes in making masters. A metal master can usually be produced for less than a hundred dollars. The master is then used to press counterfeits. Counterfeiting tapes of music as well as hit movies is easy with modern technology. The original need only be inserted into a master player, blank tapes inserted into copying machines, and the copies of film or music are produced quickly and with only minimal loss in quality.

Early laws involving counterfeiting audio or visual recordings had only minor penalties attached to them, making the offense a misdemeanor under an obscure section of the General Business Law. As a result of these early investigations, which showed links to organized crime, along with continuing lobbying efforts by the manufacturers and their trade associations, many states increased the penalties, upgrading the crime to a felony. Federal law changes increased the penalties as well, and now both federal and local laws

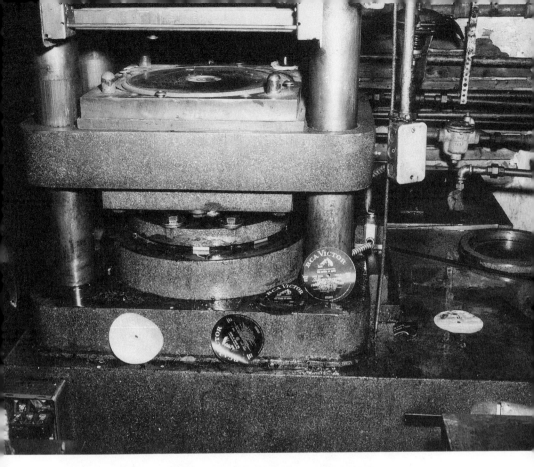

*Counterfeit phonograph record labels and record-stamping
machine found in a raid by Racket Squad detectives*

are in place to deal with counterfeiters. However, these
crimes are a relatively low priority among law enforcement
authorities swamped with serious violent crimes.

Record pirates turned to "bootlegging," a term used in
the record trade to mean the distribution of unauthorized
copies of artists' works. An unauthorized recording is made
of a concert performance. The recording is turned into a
master and the bootleg is sold, often for many times the
price of commercially available renditions by the same artist.
Some fans of popular artists want all editions of the musi-
cian's output and will pay any price for a limited bootleg

recording, even though in the end it hurts the integrity of their idol's work.

One record industry official said, "If it's a hot item and not something a company is dumping because it's overstocked, you can bet the bargain is a counterfeit. There's no such thing as the sale prices some of these record stores offer. Even the biggest record stores can't buy legitimate discs or tapes for those prices. These stores buy some legal ones to cover themselves with invoices; the rest are pirates."

The official went on to describe how some counterfeits had been discovered by manufacturers. "Record stores have return privileges," he said. "If an item doesn't sell, the stores can send it back to the manufacturer for credit. A lot of the stores bought counterfeits. When they didn't sell, the stores returned them to the manufacturers. In some cases the manufacturers' warehouses didn't know the difference. Some of the counterfeits were even repackaged and sent out again," the official said. Some counterfeits are so perfect that it requires an expert from the manufacturer's engineering department to tell the difference.

COUNTERFEIT WATCHES

Even experts have a hard time telling a counterfeit item from the real thing. Detectives from the New York City Police Department's Pickpocket and Confidence Squad seized counterfeit Omega watches from a street peddler. The detectives brought them to the Rackets Bureau. Examination revealed that the watches were stamped with 18-karat gold hallmarks along with the manufacturer's trademark insignia and name.

Police Inspector Paul Vitrano, the commander of the DA's Racket Squad, assigned one of his detectives to the case. The Pickpocket and Confidence Squad detective looked at the counterfeit Omega wristwatches. The newly assigned detective checked his own watch, a gold Omega Seamaster.

The detective looked a little sheepish. "I know those phonies," he said confidently. "I compared mine with one in a jeweler's window," he added. The detective removed his own watch and the back was snapped open with a penknife. It was clear the watch was only a good counterfeit. The case was cleverly gold plated and falsely stamped 18K. The watch stem and crown bore the raised Omega trademark and crest. The detective's watch, like the other counterfeits, was a cheap imitation. Instead of a watch worth several hundred dollars, the detective possessed a three-dollar movement in a gold-plated brass case. The only thing that was made of genuine material was the cowhide band, and that too bore a counterfeit Omega trademark, the imprint of the fine Swiss watchmaker.

The detective, like any consumer, was disappointed. Not only was he mad that he owned a phony, he was embarrassed at not recognizing it himself. His wife had bought the watch for him as an anniversary present and spent $150 for it at a shopping mall. The detective didn't have the heart to tell her she had been taken.

The con is repeated thousands of times every day. While there are several variations, it has the same general ploy. Often Italian nationals with underworld connections in Italy come to New York or other large United States cities. They make contact with people whose names were given to them in Italy and are put to work selling illegal counterfeit

Counterfeit Omega watch, along with hundreds of hallmarks seized by the police. The hallmarks were placed on fake watch faces.

watches. Their pitch goes something like this: "I am an Italian seaman. I brought this Omega watch through customs. I need money and will sell it for a good price." Sometimes, a street peddler will offer a counterfeit watch, intimating that it is stolen; in some cases street peddlers offer a tray of watches to holiday shoppers.

However the con is played, buyers quickly recognize the names Omega, Rolex, Patek Philippe, and Piaget, with their impressive gold hallmarks. The shoppers think they are getting a bargain at $75 to $150. Genuine watches by these Swiss watchmakers can cost thousands, especially for gold-and-diamond studded models. The con artist takes what the traffic will bear, sometimes getting as much as $300 to $1,500 for a particularly good imitation encrusted with jewels.

Counterfeit watch movements are often smuggled through customs from Taiwan, free ports in the Virgin Islands, or from Europe. The counterfeits the Racket Squad uncovered were assembled in New York using hand tools to imprint the false trademarks and gold hallmarks. Counterfeit crests, crowns, stems, and stamps were added, as were markings on the watch faces.

One gang, afraid to trust the watch movements to their workshop, rented a large safety deposit box in a bank vault. When our detectives finally raided the vault, armed with a search warrant, the senior bank guard remembered for years having to help a little old lady lift the heavy safe deposit box to a private booth once a week. The little old lady was the widow of a famous gangster, and the large and very heavy safety deposit box contained hundreds of smuggled watch movements. No telling who was more pleased at the apprehension, the bank guard with a weak back or Federation of Swiss Watchmakers' authorities and Interpol, who felt the Racket Squad had cracked a major Swiss watch counterfeiting network.

But Steal My Good Name

A senior executive at Bristol-Myers, the pharmaceutical company, put it succinctly when he described the value of a trademark or service mark. "The individual Alka-Seltzer tablet costs nothing to make, or the cost is negligible. Other companies can and do make fizzy tablets containing aspirin that produce the same effects as ours. Few people buy the other brands or generic "no-name" tablets. Reliance on the name Alka-Seltzer and the reputation we've developed over years of expensive advertising is what makes Alka-Seltzer sell," he said.

To paraphrase Shakespeare: "He who steals my purse steals trash, but steal my good name . . ." This is the essential complaint of product manufacturers who suffer harm from counterfeiters. Counterfeiting does not only include items like watches or records and tapes. Widespread counterfeiting of automotive and aircraft parts has been uncovered, as has the counterfeiting of drugs and pharmaceutical products. There is the risk of serious accident and even death when defective and inferior parts are substituted for reliable ones on fast-moving vehicles or aircraft. Buildings constructed with inferior parts, such as weak bolts or rivets, can cause disastrous results when exposed to the stresses and weights established for quality-controlled and tested parts. In the case of drugs, counterfeiting brand names can result in fatalities when sick and recuperating patients are treated with substitutes. The criminal associated with organized crime will sell anything that finds acceptance in the marketplace. Investigations even revealed false gold hallmarks stamped on religious medals.

Some countries, notably Taiwan, have no laws protecting trademarks. Visitors to these countries are often amazed at the shelves full of Parker pens, Ronson lighters, and the assortment of first-run motion pictures available on tape at incredibly low prices. The items are counterfeits and they often find their way out of Taiwan into the mainstream of international commerce. Customs inspectors will confiscate counterfeit brands they discover being brought into the United States, but smuggling is not easily controlled where millions of travelers cross national borders each day.

Counterfeited and falsely marked jewelry is not easy to discover. One jewelry wholesaler, having trouble moving a line of merchandise, sent the 18K-marked items to a refiner to have them melted down and the gold returned. When the refiner returned the gold to the jeweler, instead of the four kilograms of pure gold that the jeweler expected, only one and a half kilograms was produced. The jewelry wasn't nearly as pure gold as the 18K mark indicated. Expert appraisal is really the only way to verify gold purity.

Counterfeit watches, falsely stamped jewelry, and guns seized by the police

Counterfeiting is not new to the world marketplace. Bob Marx, a marine archaeologist who excavated the lost city of Port Royal, Jamaica, buried beneath the sea in a violent earthquake in 1692, discovered many falsely stamped "official" scale weights, each bearing a government hallmark certifying its accuracy. Even in early British guild halls, there was ample evidence of counterfeiting guild members' marks. Ruins from early civilizations the world over reveal wily ways in which counterfeiters have devised schemes to cash in on the good name and reputation of established makers of fine products. Official vigilance is only a partial solution. Continued pressure and lobbying by big names including Pierre Cardin, Emilio Gucci, Levi Strauss, the Federation of Swiss Watchmakers, the Jewelers' Security Alliance, the Recording Industry Association of America, and others will go a long way to assure that laws on the books will be enforced against violators. As in most things in life, those who seek a "bargain" Rolex watch or Gucci bag will find it, but often the bargain is a scam, the product of organized crime's counterfeiters, who take in millions each year fooling those made gullible by their own greed.

6

MEDICAID: THE GREAT RIP-OFF

It began with an anonymous letter, clear and to the point. The writer stated that two dentists were ripping off the Medicaid system by submitting claims for services never performed. The investigation that followed took several years and the review of millions of documents. It revealed massive organized fraud that resulted in the loss of billions in taxpayer money every year.

Medicaid, begun in 1966, is a program of free health care for persons unable to pay for it. Medicare is a program designed to provide health care assistance to older Americans on Social Security, regardless of their means to pay for it. Both programs allow recipients choice of provider, meaning they can select any doctor, dentist, chiropractor, nursing home, hospital, or pharmacy they please.

Ten years after the Medicaid program was put into action, the inspector general of the Department of Health, Education, and Welfare reported that Medicaid losses for that year alone amounted to $2.5 billion out of a total expenditure of about $9.8 billion. The same report put Medicare losses at $2.2 billion out of a $21.9 billion program. Law enforcement officials from around the country reported that organized crime had infiltrated these health care programs. With the entry of organized crime came arson, murder, extortion, and racketeering activities that profited from poorly administered medical plans for the poor and elderly. What occurred ten years after the start of Medicaid, and what is occurring now, was not only predicted but brought to public and governmental attention by a grand jury. The grand jury not only returned indictments, but issued a report that for the first time revealed the extent of criminal activity in Medicaid programs.

"There, I think we got it all . . . close the wallet, doctor."
Richmond Newsleader © 1976, The Chicago Tribune

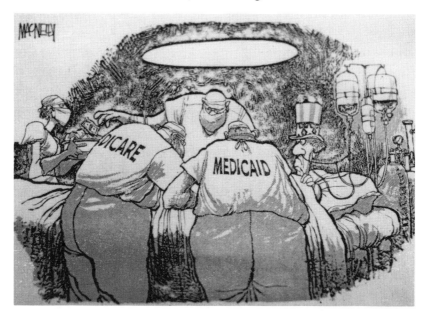

THE FIRST INVESTIGATION

Inspector Paul Vitrano, commanding officer of the district attorney's Racket Squad, had a special feeling for his detectives and their investigative techniques. Cases lasted months, even years, and the tenacity and energy of the Racket Squad detectives assigned made the difference between success and failure. The assigned detective and the DA worked as a team. The general philosophy was drawn from law enforcement in the Old West: "one riot, one ranger." Until a case needed more detectives—because physical or electronic surveillance was required—one rackets investigation usually meant one Racket Squad detective.

Detective Daniel Horowitz was assigned Medicaid. The case would involve following paper trails, tracing medical invoices and documents, and interviewing Medicaid recipients, some of whom had no permanent addresses, some with extensive criminal records. Many could not easily be found. Some were addicts or alcoholics who did not want to be found. Others were parents whose children had been mistreated by greedy medical providers. These doctors then bilked the government health care program for great profits.

When Detective Horowitz came into my office the first time to discuss the Medicaid case, little did we both know that it would take us three years and that we would open a Pandora's box of criminal activity and corruption.

The scams were vicious. They ranged from unscrupulous dentists pulling out perfectly good teeth to bill Medicaid for false teeth, to physicians who requested unnecessary tests for patients, often ones that caused pain. These tests were routinely discarded since they had not been needed in the first place. One chiropodist profited by removing the toenails

85

Val J. Halamandaris, associate counsel attached to the U.S. Senate Aging Committee poses as a Medicaid patient on the Lower East Side of Manhattan.

of terminally ill cancer patients in nursing homes. Nursing homes and ambulance services billed for dead or nonexistent patients, and they prescribed truckloads of drugs, purchased at the nursing homes' own pharmacies. The pharmacies then shorted prescriptions and overbilled. Once the unscrupulous provider had the patient's Medicaid number, all manner of services were billed to the government through a system that had no effective controls. There was no way to know what was paid and to whom, or to be able to identify chronic abusers. It was routine for providers under Medicaid to bill two to five times for the same work. Some abusers employed the services of "writers" whose only occupation was to generate Medicaid bills that the provider would send to Medicaid for payments.

Experience both in the district attorney's office in the first series of Medicaid probes, then ten years later through the United States Senate Aging Committee's investigations of Medicaid and Medicare fraud and abuse, revealed that out of the thousands of Medicaid and Medicare providers whose activities were examined, there was only one found to be totally honest. She was a medical doctor who worked for a "Medicaid mill," a storefront medical shop opened in a poor neighborhood by an entrepreneur who pulls people in off the street for all manner of health care. This medical doctor, who only worked part-time at the Medicaid mill, eventually told investigators why she refused to cheat for her boss. "I don't need the job. He needs me," she said. "I'm here to provide honest health care, and my ground rules are no cheating."

Two chiropractors who couldn't find work in their own profession were driving taxicabs in New York City at the dawn of Medicaid programs. The two stopped their cab driving to open storefront Medicaid mills in poor neighborhoods. Within a short time they were grinding out fraudulent Medicaid invoices upward of a million dollars a year. Eventually they were persuaded to turn state's evidence and reveal the extent of their and others' fraud. Under the Medicaid rip-off campaign, good medicine or health care seemed to be an accidental by-product rather than the goal of the system.

HOW THE FRAUD WAS COMMITTED

The grand jury reported that "a former high-ranking official in the Medicaid program testified that because of improper practices, 50 percent of the money spent on Medicaid went down the drain." This figure was higher than that given in the Welfare inspector general's report, which came ten years later. This kind of wholesale fraud was easy to commit. In one case investigated by the grand jury, a dentist made a false set of teeth for a patient. The patient testified that she complained to the dentist that the teeth did not fit properly. Instead of adjusting them, as the law required, the dentist made a second set of false teeth. The second set of worthless false teeth cost Medicaid another $1,500. The patient went to yet another dentist and had a third set of dentures made. Medicaid again shelled out the money. The grand jury could not obtain the appropriate records of payment because the city of New York didn't even keep a patient file. Invoices received from providers were strewn about helter-skelter, many lost, many just thrown into boxes. The city did not know whom they paid or how much, or for which patient.

Many Medicaid recipients appeared before the grand jury describing appalling examples of worthless dentures from Medicaid dentists. The patients were not paying for the services themselves, so they had little interest in the costs. They went from one doctor or dentist to another since the providers were all unsatisfactory and there was no control on how many times a patient visited them.

Dental abuses were incredible. Dentists billed for X rays, cleaning, and charting when a patient left false teeth for repair. These patients had no teeth to be cleaned, x-rayed, or charted. One dentist lost the false teeth the patient left for repair, so he billed Medicaid for making a new set. Medicaid dentists pulled out good teeth in order to bill for dentures and inflate their bills. Malpractice was rampant. A seven-year-old child had six baby teeth extracted by one dentist; the dentist had the child back six times and administered general anesthetic every time since Medicaid paid ten dollars each time. Assuming the extractions were even necessary, the teeth could have been pulled all at once. The excessive use of anesthesia on this young child created a grave health risk.

As special counsel to the United States Senate, I went under cover, posing as a buyer and "front" for certain organized crime figures interested in buying Medicaid mills. In this undercover role I made secret tape recordings for use as evidence. In one case a Medicaid mill owner, a dentist, described how he and his colleagues evaded detection. The Medicaid entrepreneur bragged: "Hurt them. . . . If you hurt them, they'll remember being treated, but they'll never know what was done." He went on to tell how his mill operated to extract optimum profits from each Medicaid patient who came through the doors.

Medicaid mills employed practitioners of all kinds, physicians, laboratory technicians, dentists, specialists, pharmacists. The pharmacy had to have a separate entranceway. The Medicaid mill owner said, "I get a deal on something. Let's say we can buy a boxcar full of a certain antibiotic cheap. You've got to get the doctors to write [the prescriptions]." The Medicaid mill owner described how he would get the doctors he hired to prescribe unnecessary drugs, sending the patients next door to his pharmacy to get the prescriptions filled.

The tape recordings revealed a range of crimes committed by Medicaid providers. In one conversation a Medicaid mill owner said, "You can make a nice buck with insurance if you feel like going that route. People have done it; don't laugh. You have to insure [the business] for a couple of hundred thousand dollars and that is it. Then if it burns, you collect your money and you are out." Medicaid mills in poor neighborhoods frequently burned—arsons committed by the owners themselves. Describing the extent of his fraudulent practices, the same Medicaid mill owner boasted, "Sure, the internist is the key to the whole thing. It is unlimited with the internist. I could actually sit down with you and, if you are really interested, show you how an internist can make so much money it is ridiculous."

Human beings meant nothing to the charlatans who operated medicine for profit in poor neighborhoods. They treated people like commodities, manipulating them for the money, choosing areas where people, because of their poverty and lack of education, were easy prey.

Unions often established medical and dental welfare plans for their members. Often these plans were bilked just as readily as public assistance. In discussing union medical plans, the Medicaid mill owner named the unions, then said, "You got to make your own connections. There are all kinds of kickbacks you can do in dentistry and medicine. I mean, there is a dental guy who makes money just off the supply business. You buy supplies from the supplier and they pay off a list price and they get a nice cash rebate on it."

It is no wonder organized crime invaded the Medicaid business. It was reaping millions. A Medicaid mill owner told me, "Listen, I was approached by a guy about three years ago who wanted to get into the medical business and I had a very nice deal for him. I had everything hooked up. Unfortunately, at the time there was a big war going on between Colombo and Gallo and the guy disappeared off the face of the earth."

The police report of a hit on a Medicaid mill doctor describes the way racketeering works best: "A person in an automobile came alongside complainant's auto and fired a shot, which took out the left front window of complainant's auto and struck complainant on the left side of the head." This mob hit, like scores of others, still remains unsolved. The psychiatrist, who was wounded, operated out of a Medicaid mill in the Bronx. The psychiatrist, in exchange for his space in the Medicaid mill, had to produce Medicaid income for the mill. He and his colleagues were also forced to use organized crime bill collectors for their Medicaid billings.

Factoring became a major abuse in the Medicaid program. Racket-connected moneylenders charged health care providers a 10 to 15 percent fee for paying their bills right away, and then collecting the full amount from New York State Medicaid, which was notoriously slow in paying. The grand jury reported: "The evidence disclosed that the advent of Medicaid gave rise to the formation of companies for the purpose of factoring Medicaid bills. Witnesses testified that a number of providers organized large Medicaid clinics that regularly submitted a tremendous volume of bills. This imposed such a burden upon the facilities of the Medicaid program that it became impossible to pay any bill properly. The long delays in payment, however, were mainly caused by inadequate record keeping and the lack of an efficient system of processing claims for payment."

The victim of the shooting described earlier was caught submitting thousands of dollars in fraudulent Medicaid billings, and he agreed to cooperate with law enforcement officials. His cooperation revealed a systematic fraud by himself and others, as well as an organized payoff scheme to New York City Medicaid officials. Testimony before the United States Congress revealed: "The bagman for these payoffs was a close associate of one Joseph Pagano, a notorious underworld mobster. [The psychiatrist] was frightened of the organized crime elements backing the Medicaid mill, and with good reason. The Medicaid mill was also used as a center for illicit drug transfers, where trucks would pick up drugs and deliver them to known mob members. . . . In those cases where bribes had to be paid at higher levels, [a certain person] would give the money to Joseph Pagano. Indeed, Pagano also took payoffs from Medicaid mill operators so there would be no union representing workers in Medicaid mills."

This testimony, based on evidence obtained during the investigations, further revealed that the operator of a Medicaid mill paid a racket boss to have someone murdered in connection with a Medicaid operation, at a time when the mill operator had some $200,000 in fraudulent Medicaid billings outstanding. Corruption was out of control. In May 1968, the New York State senator who served as chairman of the Senate Committee on Social Services and the principal backer of Medicaid legislation was indicted for perjury stemming from his testimony before a federal grand jury. Testimony before the Congress revealed that the senator's perjury was based on his "untruthfully stating that he returned $5,000 given him in May 1968 by officers of Professional Health Services, Inc., a factoring company. Other charges involved his attempt to secure the perjury of his assistant . . . and three officials of Professional Health Services, Inc." Professional Health Services and six officials of this factoring company were indicted for diverting more than $1.25 million in funds. Professional Health Services did a $12 million Medicaid factoring business each year.

The evidence revealed links between the indicted factor and many crime figures. Professional Health Services operated its own Medicaid mill. This Medicaid mill engaged in all sorts of promotions in Harlem to entice Medicaid recipients into their premises. One of their flyers read: HEALTH FAIR. JUNE 18. BRING DAD FOR FREE FATHER'S DAY GIFT. SICKLE CELL ANEMIA TEST FREE.

Evidence revealed that other Medicaid factoring companies had organized crime connections. Racketeers bilked unions by establishing health plans. The plans were designed to defraud the union welfare programs. One dental plan had its employment payrolls padded with criminals associated with organized crime. The plan operated under the auspices of the Masiello and Genovese gangs. Five known underworld bookmakers were on the dental plan's payroll.

Even a union organized to represent health care professionals, who worked in Medicaid mills, had as president a person who was under investigation in an unrelated union racketeering case that involved the attempted murder of a union candidate. Testimony before Congress about the Medicaid workers' union revealed: "It has been reported to me that [the president of the union] obtained his charter . . . by paying $10,000 to [a] New Jersey local—a union that enjoys a notorious reputation for having organized criminals associated with it. Witnesses have reported that that local [the Medicaid workers' local] was being used to shake down these doctors, to receive bribes from them so that their Medicaid mills were not organized by the union."

In all of this the patients suffered most. One mother complained that her child's teeth had been pulled out so that false bridgework could be inserted and charged to the Medicaid program. "Look at my sweet child," the mother cried, "she looks like a wolf." The young teen's appearance was ruined for life by unscrupulous Medicaid profiteers.

A skin cancer case was misdiagnosed because laboratory tests, always billed to Medicaid, were poured down the sink in a Medicaid mill.

In order to emphasize the extent of the fraud, United States senator Frank Moss, chairman of the Senate Aging Committee, agreed to pose in an undercover capacity. It was difficult for Senator Moss, from Utah, to visualize the enormity of the fraud described during the Senate committee investigation. Armed with a Medicaid card and wearing work clothes, Senator Moss went from Medicaid mill to Medicaid mill, seeing for himself the way fraudulent bills were run up. On each occasion Senator Moss, who complained of a simple cold, was asked for a urine specimen. By the third Medicaid mill, Senator Moss had no urine left. He told the mill's receptionist that he couldn't go. The receptionist sternly rebuked him, insisting that he provide a urine sample. Not knowing what to do next, Senator Moss again went into the mill's bathroom, where he saw a yellow cleaning fluid on the shelf. He took it, mixed it with water, shook it to produce a foam, and handed it in. This test, like all of the other unnecessary laboratory tests, came back "normal."

While the testimony about Senator Moss's experience made the congressmen laugh, it wasn't funny. People's serious illnesses were not being properly diagnosed. Money for medical care was being stolen and wasted. A police officer working under cover went into a Medicaid mill complaining that he felt a burning sensation when he urinated. He came out with arches in his tennis shoes.

Costs for treatments increased as Medicaid recipients were "Ping-Ponged" from one specialist to another, each time racking up maximum charges at public expense. Mu-

U.S. senator Frank Edward Moss with Senate Aging Committee investigator Val J. Halamandaris signs his Medicaid card in the U.S. Attorney's office in preparation to start his work under cover going from Medicaid mill to Medicaid mill detecting fraud.

nicipal hospitals and emergency rooms were being closed because the New York City Health and Hospitals Corporation was near bankruptcy, yet billions were being paid to charlatans who were profiting from the poor.

In one case, a child injured by an automobile was brought to a Medicaid mill. The mother brought the child back three times and each time was refused medical attention by the doctor. She was told to go to a city hospital. But the city hospital nearby had had to close its emergency room. Medicaid rip-offs had forced budget cutbacks.

In every area investigated—from the outset of the Medicaid program through the original cases in the New York DA's office to the extensive probes by the United States Senate investigating committee—it was found that criminals and racketeers were defrauding Medicaid and Medicare. Pharmacists would short-fill prescriptions, giving fewer pills than they billed for. They would alter prescriptions, changing the figure one to a four, thus billing for forty pills, instead of ten. Cheaper brands than those prescribed were dispensed. One pharmacist billed the Medicaid program for vaporizers prescribed for patients, costing $12.50 each, but gave patients inferior vaporizers that cost only $3.

Many providers defrauded Medicaid and Medicare by billing for services they did not perform. A physical therapist routinely charged for work an assistant was supposed to have performed on elderly disabled patients in nursing homes. The assistant was not even present in the nursing homes on the days for which the services were billed.

Patients were maltreated, and their health and welfare suffered as a result of the misconduct on the part of Medicaid providers. In an analysis during two years in the city of New York, the grand jury found that $136 million was spent on

Senator Moss examines medications he has just received from a pharmacy after treatment in a Harlem Medicaid center. The senator posed as a Medicaid beneficiary accompanied by his "girlfriend," Patricia G. Oriol, the chief clerk of the Senate Aging Committee.

dentistry alone. The investigative accountants found that 179 dentists, 3.8 percent of the dentists paid by Medicaid, received $49.4 million during that two-year period.

In one year alone this group of 179 dentists took in 44.3 percent of all of the money spent by Medicaid on dentistry in New York City. Three dentists took in more than $1 million each, one raking in $1.3 million; three others took in more than $750,000 in Medicaid money; and three more received in excess of $500,000 each from Medicaid. The grand jury received evidence from health department officials that a typical dentist working full-time in private practice, at that time, could earn about $60,000 a year.

Wherever money was to be made, gangsters associated

with organized crime had their front men or corporations cashing in. Racketeers took over lucrative nursing home businesses, unions in health care fields, and the factoring of Medicaid bills. As a result of the original grand jury probe and the work of the Senate committee, special prosecutors' offices were set up to investigate Medicaid and Medicare fraud. Hundreds of arrests have been made, the most recent showing that the systems are prone to the same abuses found in the original probes ten years ago. Recommendations by the grand jury were by and large ignored by government.

When New York State Supreme Court justice Jacob Grumet reviewed and released the grand jury report, revealing for the first time the extent of the fraud and abuse and the incompetence of the system to prevent it, the commissioner of the New York City Department of Social Services went on national television, standing before a bank of computers, denying that the fraud existed.

The reaction by governmental officials to revelations of widespread abuse in the programs was typical of the way people responsible for mistakes and corruption in public office behave: deny that a problem exists, then cover it up to prevent the public from discovering the extent of it. A newspaper reporter, assigned to Medicaid by a streetwise city editor, picked up on the grand jury report and the Racket Squad investigations. The *Daily News* began an investigative series. The reporter, who won a Pulitzer Prize and national attention for this investigative journalism, probably felt as frustrated as Detective Dan Horowitz and I did at the conclusion of the cases. The fraud and abuse were so widespread and rampant, the official corruption so pervasive, that we could only scratch the surface.

The United States Senate investigation had national im-

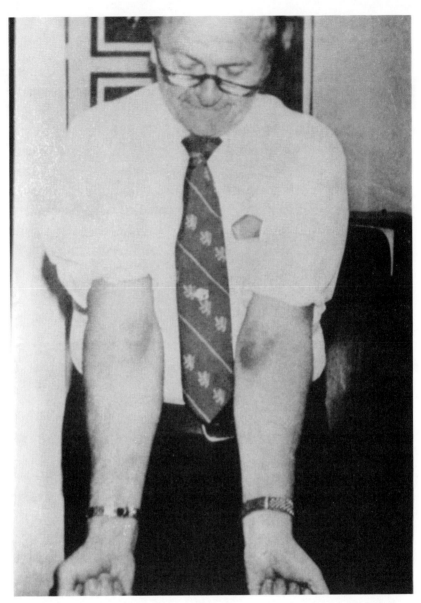

Two days after his undercover role was completed, Senator Frank E. Moss returned to Washington. Asked how he was, he replied, "Fine for someone who is sick." Here he displays bruises on his arms caused by inept blood drawing. Senator Moss has just been given his annual physical and declared in excellent health with no medical problems. "You have to experience it to believe it," Senator Moss said, describing his undercover work posing as a Medicaid patient.

99

pact, but there too, it could only scratch the surface. If there is one lesson to be learned from the Medicaid and Medicare scandals revealed by this work, it is that any program established without strict controls will not only fail to achieve its goals but will be invaded by criminals. Billions have been spent and billions have been wasted on a system that promised to provide adequate health care for all people, whether they had the means to pay for it or not. If the money wasted on Medicaid had been spent on the development of public health facilities, these would stand today as memorials to the highest standards of health care. Instead, the program has been reduced to storefront Medicaid mills operated by unscrupulous charlatans who abuse the poor for profit.

7

ON THE WATERFRONT

The docks are hard, tough places. Working the piers requires strong physical labor: stevedoring—loading and unloading ships' cargo—and handling equipment. The piers are isolated places where murder can be made to look like an accident or where a body can be dumped into the river, maybe to be found again weeks later when it floats to the surface. The cops call them floaters, the cadavers they drag out of the rivers surrounding New York's and New Jersey's waterfronts. Often the mob wants the body found. The horror of the murder can serve as an object lesson to others.

Charles "Ruby" Stein, indicted with Anthony "Fat Tony" Salerno in the loan-sharking cases, turned up dead, floating in the river, his torso dismembered, head and limbs hacked from the body before it was thrown in. Ruby Stein had served the rackets as a major loan shark and gambling boss. He had had people killed and he died as he lived, violently, on the waterfront.

Every aspect of waterfront life is controlled by organized

This victim of mob violence had been murdered, weighted with cement blocks, and thrown into New York Harbor.

crime. Unions that represent waterfront or shipboard workers have been infiltrated by gangsters and in some cases dominated by criminals associated with organized crime. Historically, the waterfront and waterborne activities were so controlled by organized crime that even during World War II, federal officials sought the help of a jailed gangster, Charles "Lucky" Luciano, in preventing espionage. When Lucky put out the word, waterfront bosses cooperated with navy intelligence, issuing union cards to counterintelligence operatives, getting them jobs on piers and boats.

The NMU Case

The National Maritime Union (NMU) was once one of the most powerful unions in the world, representing sailors and other shipboard workers. This was at the time when shipping was still important in America, before the decline of passenger liners and cargo ships. The NMU headquarters building in New York City, which now houses Covenant House, an organization for runaway young people, was once a fortress of power.

James Morrisey decided he had had enough of the bully tactics and strong-arm methods used by the union and became a reform candidate for its presidency. He was threatened but steadfastly refused to buckle. Morrisey received support from many union members, but most were afraid of retribution.

Morrisey was beaten with a lead pipe and left for dead. But he didn't die. Instead, he sought out the help of the New York district attorney's office, and with Morrisey's cooperation the DA's office began to gain the confidence of other NMU members. It learned first that union strong-arm work was contracted out to a man called D. A. Dorsey, who hung out in a bar near the NMU building.

The bar was D. A. Dorsey's office, where NMU underlings transacted business with outsiders. Dorsey also boarded ships in port and carried off the union satchel, supposedly containing only union papers, though we suspected Dorsey used the satchel to smuggle narcotics. Chief Investigator Tom Fay assigned Gerry Edwards and Leonard Muscato to infiltrate Dorsey's activities. Fay was convinced that it was Dorsey who took on the bungled contract to kill Morrisey. Investigators Edwards's and Muscato's roles were to gain Dorsey's confidence and listen in on his conversations.

While Investigator Muscato posed as a seaman, Edwards just hung out until his presence was accepted and he was in fact befriended by Dorsey. The "overheards," or conversations our investigators were able to listen in on, enabled the Racket Squad to gain warrants for wiretaps on the bar's public phone, which was used by Dorsey to transact business. The wiretaps never revealed the identity of Morrisey's assailants, although it was clear that Dorsey had taken the contract.

James Morrisey wasn't elected to the NMU's presidency, but he continued to receive threats against his life. Dorsey died as he lived. He was shot in the head while sitting on a park bench. The gun was found several feet from the body, and although the death had all the earmarks of a hit, it was put down as a suicide by the local precinct.

Soon thereafter the NMU closed the doors to its huge headquarters building. The once powerful union declined in a new era in which foreign ships with foreign crews carried on passenger service.

THE BROOKLYN CASES

The Waterfront Commission, a bistate organization with law enforcement powers, was established by compact with New York and New Jersey after evidence revealed the brutal control mobsters had on waterfront activities. Investigators from the commission conducted surveillances of waterfront gangsters. One senior investigator for the Waterfront Commission described early films they had taken of the president of the International Longshoremen's Association (ILA) meeting with a known racketeer, Heels Murphy. The investigator described how Heels shook his finger at the ILA boss, indicating mob control of the piers and the union bosses. Strong-arm tactics insured that union members did what they were told and didn't cause trouble.

There were many more subtle areas where union influence was felt. The son of the ILA union boss sold shipping containers to stevedoring companies. The commission found that the son knew nothing about containers. In hearings before the Waterfront Commission, the shipping company officials indicated that they bought the containers only because the salesman was the union leader's son.

There also were many ways the ILA could cripple the waterfront and could squeeze companies out of business. It is this absolute power, and the fear of violent retribution, that keeps the mob in control.

The Brooklyn cases didn't start at the top. They began with investigations of petty racketeering crimes, which led to the development of informants. The informants gave enough information to obtain court-authorized wiretaps and bugs. This electronic surveillance produced evidence of widespread loan-sharking, gambling, counterfeiting, smuggling, and assorted crimes including an organized theft ring that stole heavy construction equipment, like graders and bulldozers, from construction sites and brought them onto the Brooklyn piers for transshipment out of the country. Once exported, the machinery was sold at great profit.

Informants do not simply materialize. Since the risk for "ratting" on the mob is death, mobsters willing to talk usually do so when faced with the possibility of long jail sentences as the alternatives to cooperation with law enforcement. The cases against them must be strong and the potential penalties such that the risks involved in informing, either passively or actively, offer attractive alternatives.

In the Brooklyn cases there was an added problem: The

informants, knowing full well the corrupt system in New York City, absolutely refused to cooperate if their cooperation was made known to anyone connected with the Brooklyn courts or prosecution system. The informants' fears were warranted. Rackets Bureau investigations showed that there was corruption in the criminal justice system and throughout other district attorneys' offices. The informants' condition was accepted and they were assured that a special supreme court justice would be assigned who was impeccably honest, and that the formula for cooperation would be handled only through the one justice directly.

With that problem solved, the informants went to work gathering evidence, and we expanded our requests to the courts for new eavesdropping warrants. For their own protection, informants were usually only used to help a police operative get into the mob. The informant would make an introduction and vouch for the police officer, thereby eliminating the need for the informants to testify and risk danger. Some informants were relocated under the Federal Witness Protection Program, but that system had its own problems and there was the fear of eventual discovery through carelessness or corruption. A mob contract is steadfast, and the army of contract killers has been known to pursue victims to the ends of the earth.

It was on the Brooklyn court-ordered electronic interceptions that evidence was obtained involving Sonny Montella, a man the United States attorney was to use as a key witness against Brooklyn ILA union boss Anthony Scotto. It was clear from the evidence that nothing moved on the piers without ILA approval.

The FBI also had court-ordered eavesdropping on Sonny Montella and overheard the same conversations. As state officers reached out to secure the safety of a person whose life was in jeopardy, according to the conversations recorded, the FBI moved in as well. The United States attorney requested the state prosecution be delayed until the FBI investigation could be concluded.

We agreed to cooperate with the United States attorney and held off certain aspects of our investigations in Brooklyn on his promise of turning Montella and their eavesdropping evidence over to us once their case against Scotto was finished.

Anthony Scotto, the ILA boss, had connections with most every politician in the state and many in high federal public office. He could deliver votes and the union's labor endorsement, and he could deliver cash. An aspect of the federal case centered around Scotto's donating cash in ten-thousand-dollar amounts to the Democratic campaigns of public officials, including top officials in New York.

Scotto was convicted on federal racketeering charges in a sensational trial that saw a New York governor and a bevy of government officials testify on his behalf.

There are few areas of activity that are as completely and absolutely controlled by criminals as the waterfront. The United States owes its strength, its greatness, to waterborne commerce. Immigrant labor found jobs on the piers and were exploited by the old Black Hand Society, a gang of thugs who preyed on Italian immigrants. Gangs cut across ethnic backgrounds from the Irish mob to the Jewish mob to the Italian-American racketeers. The piers and waterfront activities are still dominated by organized crime and probably always will be. Unions mean political clout and money, and politicians seeking election, especially from the urban clubhouses around the ports of New York and New Jersey, are subject to the influence mob power and money can buy. If a labor racketeer like Anthony Scotto can obtain command performances by New York's governor, what chance could opposition candidate Morrisey have had in his struggle to rid his own union of thugs? It is not a question but rather an observation of life on the waterfront, where little has really changed since shape-up bosses beat vulnerable immigrant laborers into submission to their will. What *has* changed is that mobsters have become more sophisticated and working conditions have improved with the times.

8

TOXIC WASTES

Jim Kralik is a large man. He was the sheriff's chief of patrol. His Stetson, six-gun, and sheriff's star filled the doorway to the office in the Organized Crime Task Force. He came to talk.

His deputies had observed toxic and other wastes being improperly dumped into a local landfill. They had conducted surveillances. The sheriff's earlier investigations into improper dumping of wastes had been stopped. But this time the story had been covered by a local radio station, and news of the dumping had gotten out before the investigation could be squelched.

The local district attorney, politically connected to the town where the landfill was situated, was furious. The sheriff had accused the district attorney of suppressing his previous probe. Balancing the conflicting interests of two law enforcement officers, the sheriff and the district attorney, was difficult. It was important, initially, to be very methodical in reviewing the sheriff's evidence, since the district attorney clearly wanted the case shut down, stating that there was nothing to the allegations and questioning the integrity and competence of the sheriff.

"All I ask is that you look at the evidence yourself. Give the facts a fair hearing," the chief of patrol said. That was all he and the sheriff wanted. The large man wearing the sheriff's star brought with him a refreshing sense of honesty. After that first meeting with Chief James Kralik, every overture, threat, or innuendo made by the district attorney would be weighed in the light of the evidence, the integrity of the deputies who produced it, and their bosses, the sheriff and his patrol chief.

The investigation into organized crime's takeover and control of toxic waste disposal, carting, and landfilling and the role of corrupt public officials had begun in an unmarked sheriff's patrol car with deputies making observations at a rural upstate New York town garbage dump. The elements of corruption—mob ownership of some of the largest carting, waste management, and private sanitation concerns in the nation, mob murders, arson, and mob influence at the highest levels of government—would only be revealed after years of painstaking investigation, investigations made possible because of the physical and moral courage of the sheriff's detectives who sat in that unmarked car.

THE CASE THAT STARTED IT ALL

The Ramapo Mountains are a sprawling, beautiful wilderness area with large tracts still owned by a family that can trace its history back to the origins of America. Native Americans and mountain people have lived in Ramapo's forests, and the beauty of the area is one of New York State's environmental assets.

The town of Ramapo in Rockland County required expansion of its sanitary landfill to dispose of the town's solid wastes. The town threatened to seek eminent domain condemnation proceedings against the Ramapo Land Company, owner of the property where the dump was to be placed. The town prevailed, against the owner's protests. In this beautiful area, underground aquifers supply well water to residents in nearby communities. A river flowing near the site of the garbage dump supplies communities downstream with drinking water. But the deal was done and a man obtained the contract from the town to operate the dump.

There was bound to be trouble. The dump site was far too valuable a commodity to be left alone. Space for dumping garbage was at a premium in New York, and racketeer-dominated private sanitation companies had to pay to dispose of the trash they picked up from their commercial, as opposed to residential, stops. Overtures were made to the Ramapo dump operator by people connected with organized crime. The dump operator refused to allow these criminals access to the dump—until his home was set on fire. It was a clear case of arson. The arson investigator for the fire department discovered that accelerant had been used to start the fire in two different locations in the dump operator's home. In spite of the evidence, the police department in the town in New Jersey where the dump operator lived called the fire accidental and closed their investigation. The dump operator sold out, and two brothers, Carmine and Salvatore Franco, took over the operation of the Ramapo landfill.

Everyone knew what was going on. Racketeers had control of carting and now they were taking over the dump sites and landfills. This also included a firm grip on the Teamsters union, the labor organization that represented drivers of garbage trucks. At about this time the federal government was beginning to wake up to the peril of toxic wastes and the uncontrolled dumping of dangerous industrial and chemical substances, including laboratory and hospital wastes. The danger to human and animal health and the environment had been apparent for quite a while, but government was slow to act. There were many political and economic reasons for not taking action sooner. The Resource Conservation and Recovery Act (RCRA) had been passed by the United States Congress, mandating tight controls on the disposal of toxic wastes. New laws required proper disposal of waste, but there were few businesses at the outset able to do it. Enter organized crime. The toxic waste disposal racket was by far the most lucrative of all of their waste disposal businesses. It was as lucrative as the drug traffic, without any of the risks.

It was one of those coincidences that sometimes happen. The right sheriff was in office. Seventy-year-old Raymond Lindeman was not a man to be told to back off from an investigation he thought was important, and his chief of detectives, Lieutenant Stan Greenberg, was one of the best investigators in the state. They knew they had evidence of something very important. The surveillances showed the goings and comings of trucks into the Ramapo landfill, dumping all manner of things from liquids to garbage from other counties. But it was difficult, at the very beginning, to say how much of a case the investigators had.

The local county district attorney had had his hand forced. Once the case got in the news, if the story of the sheriff's report of the DA's suppression of a previous probe of improper dumping got out, he would be in a bad political position.

Since its creation, the Statewide Organized Crime Task Force (OCTF) had been used in New York to stifle politically sensitive investigations. The state investigators cooperated with local district attorneys and ducked investigations by saying an independent agency, the OCTF crime task force, had reviewed the case and found no evidence of wrongdoing. It was clearly accepted practice and everybody in the political arena knew it. That was the reason Stetson-wearing, six-gun-toting sheriff's chief of patrol Jim Kralik came by— to ask that I look at the evidence objectively.

One thing was clear: The only way to begin was to follow trucks and trace them back to the source, film and photograph where and what they picked up, then discover ownership of the carting companies. Lieutenant Stan Greenberg became known by his trademark, a Mickey Mouse T-shirt. Garbage trucks communicated by sophisticated radios, and the signals went up and down the pike from New York to New Jersey. "Mickey Mouse is on the fill," the radios would blare, and sheriff's deputies in their unmarked cars along the highways would see whole convoys of garbage trucks turn around and head back to their transfer stations for further orders.

It was dangerous work, tailing the large trucks. In one case sheriff's deputies in their police vehicle were forced off the road by a waste hauler intent on getting away. A police officer was lured into an alley blocked off by two garbage trucks and confronted by the waste haulers, a shotgun pointed at his head. Murders were being committed by mobsters in order to insure their absolute control of private sanitation and carting. Owners of toxic waste disposal companies were forced out, their companies taken over by racketeers. Those who didn't want to turn their businesses over to the mob were threatened at gunpoint.

In the light of the violence toward police personnel, we

requested 100 percent enforcement of all applicable laws, regulations, and vehicle and traffic codes. Sheriff's deputies were stationed at the Ramapo landfill and elsewhere in Rockland County. Every violation, whether for an uncovered load, a defective taillight, or a moving violation, was ticketed. At the same time the officers were obtaining positive identification of the drivers.

The surveillances paid off. The Ramapo landfill charged fees for dumping, and it was only to receive garbage from local area households. Evidence revealed that immediately upon the Francos' takeover, their company's New Jersey garbage trucks began dumping there, as did trucks containing waste collected in Westchester County, New York.

It costs a lot of money to dump garbage, seventy dollars or more a truckload. A carting company with ten to hundreds of daily loads stands to gain a great deal if it can save dump fees.

Sheriff's deputies reported observing liquid waste going into the fill, evidence of toxic contamination. The Ramapo landfill was leaching directly into nearby drinking water well systems, causing widespread contamination of the drinking water and water resources.

The carting company from Westchester was controlled by people with organized crime ties. Landfill owner Carmine Franco himself, along with several others, including Tino Fiumara, was named in a complaint arising from a landfill scandal in New Jersey. Fiumara had also been indicted in connection with the FBI ports investigation of Anthony Scotto, the International Longshoremen's Association (ILA) boss.

Everything was coming together. Two separate and apparently unrelated investigations were being conducted at the time that began to tie into the toxic waste investigations. One involved the Brooklyn organized crime gang, which used the piers to ship out stolen, heavy earth-moving equipment, discussed previously. Another involved the murder of a lottery vending machine entrepreneur in Queens, New York. The type of gun and the style of the murder of the lottery operator matched mob murders of carting company bosses in New Jersey.

As mentioned earlier, court-ordered electronic surveillance in the Brooklyn cases led to a connection with Sonny Montella. He was intimately involved in the FBI's Anthony Scotto investigation.

Everything was happening very quickly on all fronts. Two New Jersey State Police detectives were recruited to help. They made surveillances on their side of the river and cooperated with New York officers. Corruption was so rampant in New Jersey that the detectives would not turn in their files, but kept them locked in the trunks of their cars. We began developing informants, a difficult job indeed, since they knew the price they would have to pay for their cooperation if the mob found out.

But the small team of sheriff's detectives and police investigators was making good progress. Surveillances revealed that the investigation of the Ramapo landfill was causing the mob great inconvenience and they were seeking out other dump sites. At the same time surveillances at a major chemical waste disposal company in Elizabeth, New Jersey, as well as elsewhere, were providing important evidence.

Chemical Control Company was located on a peninsula of land in New Jersey between the Arthur Kill and the Elizabeth River. It was a strategic location, environmentally, since the waterways fed major tributaries that flowed into the Atlantic Ocean. Secret dumping of chemical wastes into the waterways could easily go unnoticed, but the team began to focus here since it was clear that Chemical Control was the site of major toxic waste activity.

Toxic wastes from Chemical Control were turning up all over the eastern seaboard. Investigations centered on William Carricino, head of Chemical Control, and the activities of Harold Kaufman, former Teamster sanitation union official involved with toxic wastes, as well as major organized crime figures in New York and New Jersey responsible for illegal toxic waste disposal. Pictures taken of the Chemical Control dump site when New Jersey State Police executed warrants on the premises showed a disaster area. The most deadly chemicals known were strewn about in broken, deteriorated, and leaking barrels. Poisons were stored next to leaking barrels of waste acid. Federal bomb disposal experts had to be called upon to remove explosive materials. Hospital laboratory wastes and vials of dangerous substances were strewn about the yard, and chemicals had been poured and were leaking directly into the Elizabeth River.

The photographs I took would become key evidence later on. For now, New Jersey's state officials took over the dump site and hired contractors to "clean" it up. What transpired next shows the brazen nature of the criminals involved in toxic wastes. Instead of cleaning up the Chemical Control site, chemicals and barrels of waste continued to be brought onto the premises. Mountains of dangerous and deadly wastes overflowed the street and yard. Other Chemical Control wastes had been transferred to another illegal dump under surveillance on Staten Island, New York. There, a man fronting for organized crime had taken over a bulk fuel

*An aerial view of a Staten Island, New York, toxic waste
dump site created by members of organized crime*

oil storage site with 900,000 gallon tanks and underground
pipes running into the Arthur Kill. This Chelsea-Positive oil
storage facility was on a federally protected marshland next
to the Arthur Kill waterway, upstream from a power plant.

The New York City chief of detectives cooperated, providing video surveillance equipment as organized crime task
force investigators began to monitor activities at the Chelsea-
Positive site. Chemical tankers and dump trucks rumbled in
and out. Barrels of toxic wastes were piled up, and the huge
fuel oil storage tanks were being filled with toxic wastes.
The site was owned by Texaco, but the fuel oil storage tanks
had been condemned as unsafe. The renter had been au-
thorized to use the land for packaging goods only, but packaging was far from the criminals' minds. With pressure on
Ramapo landfill, then Chemical Control, the convenience
and strategic location of the Chelsea-Positive site made it a
prime toxic waste dumping area. The underground pipes led

directly into the Arthur Kill, and the swampy marshland and creek provided perfect cover for the dumping of toxic chemicals.

The Elizabeth police chief received information that deadly chemical substances were leaking on Chemical Control premises. He sought out William Carricino, the former operator, who reluctantly went with the chief to the building. Wearing protective clothing, investigators entered Chemical Control's premises and reported to Carricino what they saw. Even Carricino was frightened. What the men reported leaking were deadly insecticides that had been there when Carricino had control of the premises, substances that had been reported "disposed of" under the New Jersey State takeover of the site.

The immediate danger was apparent, and it was clear evidence of the continued criminal use of the facility as an

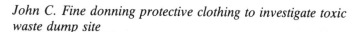

John C. Fine donning protective clothing to investigate toxic waste dump site

Aerial photograph of Chemical Control Company fire in Elizabeth, New Jersey. Thousands of barrels of deadly toxic wastes still smolder, their poisons draining into the Elizabeth River and the Arthur Kill.

illegal chemical dump. All of this revealed corruption in government. None of this could occur without the cooperation of government officials.

What happened next illustrates the way organized crime operates in the United States. Chemical Control Company in Elizabeth exploded in flames. Fireballs shot skyward like mushroom clouds. The entire eastern seaboard was lit up by the chemical fires that raged out of control, spewing deadly fumes into the atmosphere. Fireboats and fire companies poured tons of water onto the flames, flushing the residue of the deadly toxic wastes and chemicals right into the Arthur Kill and the Elizabeth River.

Even the raging inferno could not conceal the evidence. Thousands upon thousands more barrels of toxics had been brought into the Chemical Control Company site after the state of New Jersey took it over. The fire at Chemical Control was not accidental. It was deliberately set to prevent authorities from obtaining evidence of the fraud and of the official corruption that had allowed it to go on.

Search warrants were issued upon the Chelsea-Positive dump site on Staten Island. The evidence there was clear, as clear as the evidence at Chemical Control. The documents seized, and wastes and vehicles observed on the site, presented powerful proof of the illegal trafficking in toxic chemical and industrial wastes. Both sites had been taken over by people associated with organized crime.

Criminals associated with organized crime were charging industries from fifty to five hundred dollars and more per barrel to pick up and allegedly dispose of the toxic waste

Land view of Chemical Control Company, which looks like a war zone after the explosion and fire. These photographs corroborated the former operator's testimony that thousands more barrels of toxic waste were brought onto the site after government authorities took it over, ostensibly to clean it up.

properly. What they were doing was dumping it into the ocean, river tributaries, or landfills. At the Chelsea-Positive dump site we found new evidence, confirming what we had been told. The mob was mixing PCBs (polychlorinated biphenyls—cancer-causing chemicals used in transformers), waste oils, and other flammable toxic chemicals with home heating fuels. This was at the height of the fuel oil crisis, when prices for gasoline and home heating oil had skyrocketed.

Underground fuel tanks at the Chelsea-Positive tanks were filled with toxic wastes, and they were leaking. Hoses were everywhere, leading into the marshland, confirming that there was massive illegal storage and dumping of toxic wastes.

Evidence led to Long Island, New York, and into northern New York State, where organized crime figures had taken over dump sites and where more illegal disposal of toxic wastes was occurring. There was pressure to curtail the investigations. The arrests and police raids were receiving widespread publicity, and the focus of the probes began to put pressure on politicians who had secret ownership in toxic waste companies. These politicians were in league with gangsters. Many politicians received campaign contributions from the gangsters or their companies. There were warnings from reliable sources that the investigations were being sabotaged and the cases fixed.

The toxic waste cases were building to a crescendo. The Special Grand Jury for Investigations into Organized Criminal Activities in Rockland County returned a seventy-nine-page report. The report detailed the local menace of toxic waste contamination of land and water resources as well as the overall problem throughout the United States.

The author takes samples of PCB-laden waste oil spread on a country road by criminals while a worried mother asks about the future health of her children, who had been playing in the oil and putting rocks from the road into their mouths.

The grand jury report resounded like a rifle crack across the country. It took the federal government to task and for the first time outlined the enormity of the problem and the lack of effective controls. It reported: "Environmentally unsound, dangerous, illegal, and deliberately improper practices in generating, transporting, treating, storing, and disposing of hazardous wastes and solid wastes by certain elements have contaminated the land and water, caused disease, including birth defects, mutations in children, cancer, miscarriages, liver damage, and other diseases, leading to death and degeneration of human and animal health, and have created irreversible damage to elements of the environment. These improper and dangerous practices are flagrant and widespread."

122

The report continued: "The evidence further disclosed the inability of government agencies at all levels to deal effectively with the problems presented by deliberate and improper waste disposal practices in the past."

Evidence was obtained by the grand jury from a high-ranking official of the United States Environmental Protection Agency (EPA), who testified: "Over 90 percent of the hazardous waste generated in the United States today is handled improperly and may be or is causing detrimental effects to human health and the environment every day."

Attempts were made to interfere with the grand jury, as politicians exerted pressure. The grand jury reported, with regard to the EPA, that "policymakers at the highest level of the EPA instructed their personnel not to seek out sites that may pose serious hazards to human beings or the environment. . . ."

State officials from the Bureau of Hazardous Waste were quoted by the grand jury report as saying that New York had a "nonsystem for the control of hazardous wastes," and the bureau had not been involved in investigating violations in that area.

The grand jury spoke in legal but tough language when it concluded that "the evidence indicates the response of federal, state, and local governments to the problems posed by hazardous waste has been characterized by ignorance, neglect, laxity, and fractionalization of responsibility."

Anthony Scotto, the waterfront union boss, had been convicted of federal racketeering charges. A parade of political big shots had testified in Scotto's behalf. At this point the federally protected witness, Sonny Montella, along with all of the FBI's wiretaps, was available. Tape recordings of conversations with a member of the state assembly Hazardous Waste Committee revealed that testimony before the committee about organized crime's role in the toxic waste area had been put off for a year to protect Scotto from being linked with Tino Fiumara and others.

Official testimony before the New York Assembly had been put off, the toxic waste and political corruption investigations sabotaged and squelched, and then my office in the Organized Crime Task Force was burglarized and searched in the hopes of finding tape recordings of the evidence. The New York attorney general's chief for criminal matters was told that warnings were received that were relative to the investigations being fixed. That proved to be a mistake.

In a further attempt to intimidate, death threats were issued against me, stating a contract had been put out on my life.

During the course of investigations into criminal dumping of toxic wastes, repeated requests were made to New York State Police officials to monitor trucks carrying liquid and solid wastes. The state police had special weighing units on the highways where trucks had to stop and drivers could be identified. No reports were received from them, although continuous requests were made. The matter was discussed during meetings with New York State Police superiors, environmental officials, and the district attorney of Orange County. Still nothing.

As it turned out, the State Investigation Commission had a long-term investigation into the activities of the state police involving organized payoff schemes with truckers. The New York Senate Committee on Toxic Wastes took up the investigation into the illegal disposal of toxic wastes and organized crime's takeover of toxic waste disposal and hauling concerns and landfills. In these investigations, I wore a concealed tape recorder to gather evidence by talking with a toxic waste truck driver. The driver said it was routine for toxic waste concerns to falsify drivers' log books and cause drivers to exceed the maximum driving hours per day regulated by the Department of Transportation. Drivers carrying dangerous, often deadly, cargoes of hazardous and toxic wastes were cutting safety corners on the roads. I learned that a concern under investigation in Bayonne, New Jersey, had been dumping directly into the Arthur Kill. The driver often delivered and picked up from there.

The company involved had sewage sludge hauling contracts with New York City, and the information revealed that this waste was mixed with toxics and the lot dumped into the waterways surrounding New York. A principal of the company was appointed ports and terminals commissioner of the city of New York even though the company had been under investigation and was cited for violations of the law. Eventually a barge captain who had worked for this company for fourteen years gave evidence of massive illegal dumping. He witnessed the death of dolphins and whales that swam through the stream of waste his boat released in the ocean.

The Senate investigation revealed that the Chelsea-Positive dump site cleanup work had been given to a person and company under investigation as an illegal dumper. The evidence further revealed that this company took wastes from Chelsea-Positive and illegally dumped them into a New York City landfill on Staten Island. Evidence disclosed that the owner had been bribing New York City officials, and it was through this corruption that they were allowed to dump dangerous toxic wastes into the city landfills.

With the cooperation of Long Island, New York, police and the prosecutor's office, search warrants were executed

125

on a number of toxic waste outfits on Long Island. The evidence was mounting; it was clear that organized crime not only dominated carting, but had a stranglehold on every aspect of waste collection, disposal, and treatment. William Carricino, the former owner of Chemical Control Company, cooperated with the Senate committee. The committee also secured evidence from the former Teamsters sanitation union official Harold Kaufman, who was now in the Federal Witness Protection Program hiding out with a new identity. The evidence coming from inside confirmed what had been revealed before the legislative investigative committees all along.

Carricino reported that Chemical Control Company had been taken away from him at gunpoint. One John Albert and other hoodlums approached him; a gun was thrust into his stomach and he was given a choice: get out or die. Carricino got out. He testified to the amount of toxic wastes he left behind. Carricino swore that he made a number of calls to the New Jersey attorney general's office to report criminal activity in dumping toxic wastes, hoping to offer his cooperation. Each time he then received a call from a person associated with organized crime who threatened him, warning him to stay away from authorities.

New Jersey officials tried to discredit Carricino, for if he was to be considered truthful, then it was clear that corruption reached the highest levels of New Jersey state and local government. Carricino was jailed for violations of the dumping laws. What the corrupt New Jersey officials never counted on were my photographs taken both before and after the explosion of Chemical Control Company in Elizabeth. The pictures showed the buildup of toxic wastes, not only confirming Carricino's testimony but showing the extent to which corrupt government will go to cover up their misconduct.

Harold Kaufman was a bird of a different feather. Kaufman was steeped in organized crime, having been associated with racketeers for many years. Kaufman's testimony was a startling revelation of how organized crime works. Describing the indictments that had been returned by the special grand jury in Rockland County, indictments that had been dismissed by a county judge, who was an admitted friend of Ramapo town officials, Harold Kaufman wrote: "After more than two years secretly taping the Mafia, which was insidiously spreading its interests from the garbage industry into the more lucrative toxic waste dumping business, it was time for me to drop out of circulation—before it was too late. I had been associated with the mob for more than a dozen years, spent time with them in prison before that. . . . Maybe it was my conscience. Maybe I suddenly got religion. But toxic waste isn't loan-sharking or gambling or even narcotics. It's a whole lot deadlier. And the Mafia got into it in the 1970s because of the enormous profits from midnight dumping."

The legislative committee that compelled Harold Kaufman's testimony about the Ramapo landfill reported: "Carmine Franco, a member of the Genovese/Tieri crime family, took over the Ramapo landfill contract in 1976. Franco was already heavily involved in the garbage hauling business in New Jersey and was president of the New Jersey Trade Waste Association, which was later found guilty of illegally monopolizing the garbage industry in that state. Franco and his partner, Anthony Rizzo, were sentenced to eighteen months in New Jersey State Prison, but this was suspended, and they received 180 days in jail. . . ."

The investigating committee focused in on the way the investigations and the indictments against the Francos and Rizzo were fixed. Kaufman explained at this committee's hearing how he had discussed the Ramapo landfill operation with Franco and his partner, Anthony Rizzo, at a New Jersey Trade Waste Association grievance meeting, where property rights disputes were resolved.

The following testimony reveals the extent of organized crime domination in toxic waste and its corruptive influence:

CHAIRMAN HINCHEY [Maurice Hinchey, the chairman of the New York Assembly Committee on the Environment]: Do you have any knowledge of the Ramapo landfill?
KAUFMAN: Just through grievance meetings at the New Jersey Trade Waste Association, and from what Carmine Franco told me and from what Anthony Rizzo told me.
CHAIRMAN HINCHEY: What did they tell you?
KAUFMAN: That it was a gold mine. They had forced out the previous owners with threats, and they had this landfill that would take anything but the kitchen sink.
CHAIRMAN HINCHEY: There were some investigations that were going on with regard to the illegal dumping of toxic and hazardous material in parts of Orange and Rockland counties. . . . Do you know of any indictments that were pending as a result of that activity?
KAUFMAN: Yes, I do. Carmine Franco was indicted and Anthony Rizzo was indicted; and some truck drivers from both of these companies.
CHAIRMAN HINCHEY: At one point you had a conversation with Mr. Franco on that subject—and can you tell us what he told you?
KAUFMAN: Yes, sir. When I was undercover with the FBI and also the state of New Jersey at that time, I went to

the garbage convention in Atlantic City, where I met Mr. Carmine Franco, who was there, who had just beaten this charge, and the indictment was dropped. He told me money talks, and you can take it from there. . . .

CHAIRMAN HINCHEY: Did you infer from what he said that he had paid someone, and as a result of that payment, the indictment against him and other people was taken care of, if you will?

KAUFMAN: There is no doubt in my mind, that is what he was inferring, that is what he was bragging about, and that is what he was claiming.

The evidence continued to build. Corporate directors and bosses of major companies were changed until, on paper at least, the fronts for these mob-dominated companies were "legitimate" businesspeople.

Federal, state, and local officials were informed of problems and the dangers. There were meetings at the White House with the president's designees for administrator of the EPA, the deputy administrator, and the president's adviser for the environment. Some were to attain notoriety for misconduct later on, but they could never say they were not warned of the danger, the course of action they should have followed, and the potential consequences for failing to act.

The EPA in Washington received a copy of the special grand jury report detailing problems at the EPA, articles about the toxic waste problem, and enough material to convince them of the need for effective enforcement and control of toxic waste. Problems within the EPA were discussed, as was evidence of cover-ups and conflicts, as well as the fact that the states, upon whose shoulders the new EPA administrator wanted to place the burden for toxic waste control, were ill-equipped to handle the problem.

At the very outset of their administration, the top EPA administrators were informed of how companies involved with toxic waste hauling and disposal were infiltrated by racketeers, and of the high risk improper dumping posed as a threat to human health and the environment. They were told how "paper companies" were set up to conceal ownership of dump sites and thus effectively limit liability when the sites were improperly loaded with toxic wastes and abandoned. Later, in a wave of scandal, the person in charge of toxic waste for the EPA was indicted. Congressional probes revealed that EPA's toxic waste enforcement was ineffective.

Ironically, an EPA employee in charge of toxic waste danger assessments, who had been supplying us with information, had said at the outset of our investigation, "Wait a minute. Before you start on this toxic waste stuff, you better know what you're in for. They can buy a governor like that. . . ." He snapped his fingers for emphasis. With hindsight, in the light of all that has been revealed since, the EPA official's comment and cynicism probably should have served as a warning of things to come.

Toxic waste is big business, and in an area controlled by organized crime, that means bad business until the people finally demand redress. So corrupt was the political structure in New York and New Jersey that the frail efforts by citizens, risking their lives, linking their hands to prevent waste hauling trucks from entering landfills near their homes, could never succeed. Cases and investigations were fixed even before the criminals could be brought to justice. The corrupt politicians who profited from their misconduct continue to prosper, to the detriment of children still unborn and those stricken with health defects and diseases caused by greed.

BIBLIOGRAPHY

Alexander, Shana. *The Pizza Connection*. New York: Weidenfeld and Nicolson, 1988.

Block, Alan A., and Frank A. Scarpitti. *Poisoning for Profit: The Mafia and Toxic Waste in America*. New York: William Morrow, 1985.

Bresler, Fenton. *The Chinese Mafia*. New York: Stein and Day, 1981.

Brill, Steven. *The Teamsters*. New York: Simon and Schuster, 1978.

Cohen, Jerry S., and Morton Mintz. *Power, Inc.* New York: Viking, 1976.

Congdon, Thomas, and Vincent Teresa. *Wiseguys*. New York: E. P. Dutton, 1978.

DiMona, Joseph, and George Wolf. *Frank Costello: Prime Minister of the Underworld*. New York: William Morrow, 1974.

Feder, Sid, and Joachim Joesten. *The Luciano Story*. New York: David McKay, 1954.

Hoffa, James R. *Hoffa: The Real Story*. New York: Stein and Day, 1975.

Maas, Peter. *The Valachi Papers*. New York: G. P. Putnam's Sons, 1968.

Mills, James. *The Underground Empire: Where Crime and Governments Embrace*. New York: Doubleday, 1986.

Moldea, Dan E. *The Hoffa Wars*. New York: Paddington Press, 1978.

Reid, Ed. *Mickey Cohen: Mobster*. New York: Pinnacle Books, 1973.

Tuohy, James, and Rob Warden. *Greylord Justice Chicago Style*. New York: G. P. Putnam's Sons, 1989.

131

INDEX

INDEX

135

INDEX